D0849644

META-ETHNOGRAPHY:
Synthesizing Qualitative Studies

GEORGE W. NOBLIT
University of North Carolina, Chapel Hill
R. DWIGHT HARE
Northeast Louisiana University

Qualitative Research Methods,
Volume 11

SAGE PUBLICATIONS
The Publishers of Professional Social Science
Newbury Park   Beverly Hills   London   New Delhi

For information address:

SAGE Publications, Inc.
2111 West Hillcrest Drive
Newbury Park, California 91320

SAGE Publications Inc.
275 South Beverly Drive
Beverly Hills
California 90212

SAGE Publications Ltd.
28 Banner Street
London EC1Y 8QE
England

SAGE PUBLICATIONS India Pvt. Ltd.
M-32 Market
Greater Kailash I
New Delhi 110 048 India

International Standard Book Number 0-8039-3022-4
International Standard Book Number 0-8039-3023-2 (pbk.)

Library of Congress Catalog Card No. 87-22330

FIRST PRINTING

When citing a university paper, please use the proper form. Remember to cite the correct
Sage University Paper series title and include the paper number. One of the following
formats can be adapted (depending on the style manual used):

(1) IVERSEN, GUDMUND R. and NORPOTH, HELMUT (1976) "Analysis of
Variance." Sage University Paper series on Quantitative Applications in the Social
Sciences, 07-001. Beverly Hills: Sage Pubns.

OR

(2) Iversen, Gudmund R. and Norpoth, Helmut. 1976. *Analysis of Variance.* Sage
University Paper series on Quantitative Applications in the Social Sciences, series no.
07-001. Beverly Hills: Sage Pubns.

*To Mary and Jaynie who gave us
the love and support they deserved.*

EDITORS' INTRODUCTION

Reviewing a literature is a task that excites few social researchers. Most regard it as a necessary but tedious prelude to the real work of social research. Standard-form reviews usually carry a Whiggish perspective wherein the past is seen to inform the present such that a tidy accumulation of knowledge results. The idea is to record the progress in a given domain, identify the gaps and weak points that remain, and thus plot the proper course for future work. These aims are ordinarily regarded as so unproblematic and commonsensical that little else needs to be said about how a body of literature is to be treated other than to encourage the reviewer to keep it succinct and brief.

Things are hardly so straightforward in practice. As any student who has tried to write a review of some area of social research knows, standards must be invented in which to place previous work, standards must be created to evaluate this work, and a perspective must be brought to bear on the materials to give the review coherence. These are difficult matters. Moreover, as George Noblit and Dwight Hare tell us in Volume 11 of the Sage series on qualitative research methods, literature reviews done well require a good deal of originality and serious scholarship.

Meta-ethnography is about the comparative textual analysis of published field studies. The authors argue that there are at least three ways to order a set of ethnographies. First, ethnographies can be combined such that one study can be presented in terms of another. Second, ethnographies can be set against one another such that the grounds for one study's refutation of another become visible. Third, ethnographies can be tied to one another by noting just how one study informs and goes beyond another.

The form a particular meta-ethnography takes depends on the kinds of explanations used in the ethnographies studied. Some explanations are compatible across studies, some are not, and some are explanations for quite different phenomena. The comparative procedures developed in this monograph rest on the deceptively simple idea that ethnographic work cannot be understood or adequately summarized on the basis of

5

empirical results alone. Such research always presumes a social and theoretical context within which substantive findings emerge. The recovery of this context and its comparison across studies are the aims of meta-ethnography.

The achievement of such aims is no easy matter. To tackle a set of ethnographic studies with the intent of somehow ordering the diversity found within them is a demanding task for which few guidelines currently exist. This monograph offers some useful procedural advice for the comparative analysis of ethnography and does so most practically through the use of numerous examples. In essence, Noblit and Hare show us how to become more skilled and careful readers of ethnographic texts.

John Van Maanen
Peter K. Manning
Marc L. Miller

PREFACE

We are interested in how qualitative researchers interpret and explain social and cultural events. This monograph represents one line of our investigations: how to "put together" written interpretive accounts. We are also convinced that all synthesis, whether quantitative or qualitative, is an interpretive endeavor. When we synthesize, we give meaning to the set of studies under consideration. We interpret them in a fashion similar to the ethnographer interpreting a culture. We view our approach to be but one possible approach and hope other approaches will be developed.

Our approach starts from the premise that all interpretive explanation is essentially translation and argues that a meta-ethnographic synthesis is itself a reciprocal translation of studies. Viewing interpretive explanation as translation has implications for how ethnographers, interpretivists, and qualitative researchers express what they know. It means that there is an alternative to the simple accumulative logic so common in social sciences. We can retain the uniqueness and holism of accounts even as we synthesize them in the translations. It also means that qualitative researchers need to be culturally multilingual, able to facilitate discourse between cultural languages. If effective translations are to be accomplished, we must be able to render the idiomatic meanings of one culture in terms of the idiomatic meanings of another. We think this line of thought is provocative and promising, but few of us are prepared for what it asks of us as researchers and writers.

As interested as we are in the substance of this monograph, we could not have produced it without Deborah Eaker. As critic, manager, editor and friend, she gave our writing form and substance. Her knowledge and insight found and solved many problems. Her diligence reduced our carelessness. We were fortunate to have her work with us and deeply appreciate her efforts.

Susan Knight and Penny Mahorney converted illegible script to typed page and improved it in the transition. We appreciate not only their word processing, but also their defense of the priority of this manuscript and their unfailing good cheer. It has been a pleasure to work with them.

We thank Blanche Arons for her meticulous reading of the first draft. Her time and effort saved us tedious hours of technical editing.

Bill Johnston, Lynn Eisenberg, James McLaughlin, and Cheryl Southworth read and critiqued an earlier draft of the manuscript. Their suggestions greatly improved the product. As is evident in Chapter 1, Ray Rist, Murray Wax, Marki LeCompte, and the authors of the desegregation ethnographies first struggled with the issues of how to synthesize ethnographic studies and taught us both about ethnography and about the problem of synthesis. Frederick Erickson, Mary Haywood Metz and Judith Warren-Little critiqued various preliminary papers, giving shape and direction to our thinking. We thank John Van Maanen for understanding what we are about, and Peter Manning for his apt critique and guidance. Mitch Allen was unfailing with good cheer, determination, and deadlines. He also was honest about the prospects of this idea and book.

We thank all of these people for their efforts to improve our thought and writing. Any faults that remain are ours.

G.W.N.
R.D.H.

META-ETHNOGRAPHY:
Synthesizing Qualitative Studies

GEORGE W. NOBLIT
University of North Carolina, Chapel Hill

R. DWIGHT HARE
Northeast Louisiana University

Part I

INTRODUCTION

In this book, we present an argument concerning how qualitative researchers ought to think about interpretive explanation and practice the synthesizing of multiple studies. All of the books in this series share a common concern of improving the craft of qualitative research and in advancing our interpretive understanding of social phenomena. While we vary from the other books in that our concern is not so much with language or practice, but with the nature of interpretive synthesis, our efforts fully complement the other volumes.

Our approach to synthesizing qualitative studies has two primary applications. First, students and researchers are perennially involved in conducting and writing literature reviews. Our meta-ethnographic approach enables a rigorous procedure for deriving substantive interpretations about any set of ethnographic or interpretive studies. Like the quantitative counterparts of meta-analysis (Glass et al., 1981; Hunter et al., 1982) and the integrative research review (Cooper, 1984), a meta-ethnography can be considered a complete study in itself. It compares and analyzes texts, creating new interpretations in the process. It is much more than what we usually mean by a literature review. Second, qualitative researchers in the process of analyzing data create various

9

texts: notes, matrices, preliminary descriptions, and analyses. We compare these texts as we create a holistic interpretation. Our approach suggests a way to approach this comparative and interpretive task. As will become evident, synthesizing qualitative research is no simple task. It requires a sophisticated understanding of the nature of comparison and interpretation, a meticulous yet creative rendering of the texts to be synthesized, and reciprocal translations of the meanings of one case into the meanings of another. Each of these processes is addressed in this book.

While interpretivists are reluctant to define things in the abstract, we will venture what we mean by the term *meta-ethnography*. Meta-ethnography is the synthesis of interpretive research. To preserve the uniqueness and holism that characterize qualitative studies, we argue that one form of meta-ethnography involves the translation of studies into one another. The translation of studies takes the form of an analogy between and/or among the studies. Further explanation and elaboration follow.

In Part I, we advance a theory about how interpretivists might appropriately derive understanding from multiple ethnographic accounts. Chapter 1 develops the unique issue of synthesizing understanding from interpretive studies and proposes one basis, comparative explanation as translation, on which to develop a meta-ethnography. Chapter 2 discusses the phases of a meta-ethnography and translation as a form of interpretive explanation, suggesting that it may be best to think metaphorically about ethnographic narratives and syntheses.

In Part II, we discuss three different types of meta-ethnographic syntheses, give examples of these types of syntheses, and draw some conclusions. Chapter 3 discusses syntheses as reciprocal translations of each account into the other. Chapter 4 addresses the problem of synthesizing studies that are refutations of each other and presents examples that deal with this problem. Chapter 5 elaborates a third type of synthesis: the construction of a whole from studies of parts. We give an example of the lines-of-argument types of syntheses. Finally, Chapter 6 discusses the inscription of syntheses and some of the issues involved in constructing translations, creating analogies, and writing.

1. THE IDEA OF A META-ETHNOGRAPHY

Meta-ethnography is a term we use to characterize our approach to synthesizing understanding from ethnographic accounts. Our analogy here is obviously to meta-analysis (see Glass et al., 1981; Hunter et al., 1982). Any similarity lies only in a shared interest in synthesizing empirical studies. What follows is our idea about how qualitative researchers ought to think about this task. This book is not for everyone. It will be of most interest to social scientists who struggle to "put together" the many qualitative studies now being produced, to the researcher or student who wishes to construct interpretivist literature reviews, to policy researchers and policymakers who wish to use humanistic research in their deliberations but who are at a loss about how to "reduce" it, and to qualitative researchers concerned with interpreting multiple cases and/or alternative lines of argument.

We argue that a meta-ethnography should be interpretive rather than aggregative. We make the case that is should take the form of reciprocal translations of studies into one another. The need for this type of discourse is based on a concrete example of a synthesis attempt that failed. The example itself reveals why this type of discourse is needed. As argued elsewhere (Noblit, 1984), utilitarian culture places unique demands on qualitative research to be practical: Witness the growth of qualitative evaluation research. Since research and evaluation funding are tied to improvement of practice, it is especially important that interpretivists discuss how they construct explanations, how interpretive explanations are different from other ways of constructing explanations, and what can reasonably be said about some sets of studies. Despite our utilitarian culture, a meta-ethnography cannot be driven by technical interests (Habermas, 1971). Instead, meta-ethnography must be driven by the desire to construct adequate interpretive explanations. As the range of interpretive, qualitative social research expands, we will need to focus our discourse on how we might compare our accounts. This focus must occur even if, as Geertz (1973) argues, there is little prospect of creating a general theory of interpretivism. The more formal qualitative researchers (e.g., Miles and Huberman, 1984) see the issue of comparing studies as one of explicitness about the processes we use to analyze our data. We tend to agree with Marshall's (1985) assessment that this is the "bureaucratization" of data analysis. The meta-ethnographic approach we develop here takes a different tack: We focus on constructing interpretations, not analyses. To our way of thinking, the synthesis of qualitative research should be as interpretive as any ethnographic account.

The Paradigm Problem

Our notion of meta-ethnography is firmly based in the interpretive paradigm. It is an alternative to developed approaches in the positivist paradigm. *Paradigm*, as Kuhn (1970) uses the term, refers to both "the entire constellation of beliefs, values, techniques, and so on shared by the members of a given community" (p. 175), and the exemplary but "concrete puzzle-solutions" (p. 175) of the scientific community. In the social sciences, the two major paradigms are interpretivism and positivism.

The interpretivist paradigm includes research that is termed *ethnographic, interactive, qualitative, naturalistic, hermeneutic,* or *phenomenological.* All these types of research are interpretive in that they seek an explanation for social or cultural events based upon the perspectives and experiences of the people being studied. In this way, all interpretive research is "grounded" in the everyday lives of people. In doing so, interpretivists seek "to make sense of an object of study . . . to bring to light an underlying coherence" (Taylor, 1982: 153).

Interpretivist studies usually rely on "thick description" (Geertz, 1973), the detailed reporting of social or cultural events that focuses on the "webs of significance" (Geertz, 1973) evident in the lives of the people being studied. Since these studies reveal that context affects the meaning of events, interpretivists are dubious about the prospects of developing natural science-type theories or laws for social and cultural affairs.

The positivist paradigm is optimistic about the prospects for general theories or laws and largely seeks to develop them. Some positivists insist on a strict deductive logic—stating theory, deducing hypotheses, and testing the hypotheses. Others are less strict, arguing that the causal laws of social affairs can be discovered through empirical study, and through the accumulation of such studies. In general, however, positivists quantify social events and assess the statistical relationships between variables in the service of constructing an abstract theory.

Explanation in the positivist paradigm is causal and predictive (Bredo and Feinberg, 1982: 19). Positivists seek cause-and-effect laws that are sufficiently generalizable to ensure that a knowledge of prior events enables a reasonable prediction of subsequent events.

Because the positivists see knowledge as accumulating, they have been more interested in developing approaches to research synthesis than have interpretivists. A meta-ethnography fills this void by proposing a uniquely interpretive approach to research synthesis.

The Meaning of Meta-Ethnography

The intent of this book is to provide one way for interpretivists to derive understanding from multiple cases, accounts, narratives, or studies. A meta-ethnography is intended to enable:

(1) more interpretive literature reviews

(2) critical examination of multiple accounts of an event, situation, and so forth

(3) systematic comparison of case studies to draw cross-case conclusions

(4) a way of talking about our work and comparing it to the works of others

(5) synthesis of ethnographic studies

The type of thinking we propose is useful to the researcher trying to compare across case studies within a single study as well as to someone wishing to review the ethnographic literature on some area of interest. We will focus more on the latter in this book, demonstrating how interpretive studies may be reduced, compared, and translated as a way of synthesizing the studies. We use the prefix *meta* to indicate our intent to focus on the synthesis enterprise. A meta-ethnography seeks to go beyond single accounts to reveal the analogies between the accounts. It reduces the accounts while preserving the sense of the account through the selection of key metaphors and organizers. The "senses" of different accounts are then translated into one another. The analogies revealed in these translations are the form of the meta-ethnographic synthesis.

What this synthesis entails will be explained in the following chapters. In constructing these explanations, we rely on a set of terms that need some definition. Of most concern is how we distinguish between *interpretive, qualitative,* and *ethnographic*. For us, interpretive refers to the larger paradigm we have just discussed. Qualitative, for us, refers to the range of approaches practiced within the interpretive paradigm, including ethnography, case study research, intensive interviewing studies, and discourse analysis, among others. Ethnographic refers to a basic approach within interpretivism that is common to anthropologists and sociologists. Our focus here is largely on studies that define themselves as ethnographic. By this we usually mean long-term, intensive studies involving observation, interviewing, and document review (as well as review of other human products). However, in defining ethnography, we agree with Wolcott (1980: 56):

> One could do a participant-observer study from now to doomsday and never come up with a sliver of ethnography. . . . We are fast losing sight of the fact that the essential ethnographic contribution is interpretive rather than methodological.

We refer to the texts of studies created by interpretivists in various ways. Since we focus on the synthesis of ethnographic studies, we refer to these alternatively as accounts, studies, and ethnographies. Others may wish to distinguish between them, but we do not do so here.

Metaphor is a term that we develop in some detail. For now, it is important to know that when we talk about the key metaphors of a study, we are referring to what others may call the themes, perspectives, organizers, and/or concepts revealed by qualitative studies. Further, while we discuss criteria for adequate metaphors and the appropriate form of translations, we wish to be clear that, in the interpretive paradigm, any interpretation, metaphor, or translation is only one possible reading of that studied. Other investigations will have other readings.

In many ways, a meta-ethnographic synthesis reveals as much about the perspective of the synthesizer as it does about the substance of the synthesis. This is reflected in several ways in this book. First, we are concerned with an aspect of practice within the interpretive paradigm. Our audience, then, is interpretivists and students of interpretivism. Second, we are educational ethnographers. We want to know what interpretivism, ethnography, and qualitative research can reveal about the social institution of education. Therefore, most of the synthesis examples are of studies of education. Third, we are interested in understanding education in our own society. The examples that follow are about or have implications for education in the United States. Cross-cultural and cross-national studies are amenable to the same approach we develop here, as the synthesis of Margaret Mead's and Derek Freeman's studies reveal. However, it is clear that cross-cultural studies involve translation at another level (Asad, 1986). Such translation needs more consideration than we can provide in this volume, but we encourage those who conduct cross-cultural studies to undertake this task.

The meaning of meta-ethnography for us is as a form of synthesis for ethnographic or other interpretive studies. It enables us to talk to each other about our studies; to communicate to policy makers, concerned citizens, and scholars what interpretive research reveals; and to reflect on our collective craft and the place of our own studies within it.

Knowledge Synthesis

The synthesis of research for many is, no doubt, equated with doing literature reviews. Positivists and interpretivists alike find literature reviews as usually practiced to be of little value. The study-by-study presentation of questions, methods, limitations, findings, and conclusions lacks some way to make sense of what the *collection* of studies is saying. As a result, literature reviews in practice are more rituals than substantive accomplishments.

Positivists have had more interest in knowledge synthesis than interpretivists. For them, knowledge accumulates. The problem has been how best to accomplish that accumulation. Positivists have had major advances in this area in recent years. [For examples, see works on meta-analysis (Glass, 1977; Hunter et al., 1982) and integrative research reviews (Cooper, 1984).] This emphasis on accumulation of data is not an accident. Meta-analysis was designed with the presumption that there were many small-scale studies, chiefly evaluations, that gathered some common data; however, these individuals studies were too limited for reliable generalizations. Driven by a wish to overcome this problem, integrative reviews and meta-analysis guide the pooling of data from the studies, and its subsequent statistical analysis.

In applied research, meta-analysis has come to refer to a specific technique. Glass et al. (1981: 21) write:

> The approach to research integration referred to as "meta-analysis" is nothing more than the attitude of data analysis applied to quantitative summaries of individual experiments. By recording the properties of studies and their findings in quantitative terms, the meta-analysis of research invites one who would integrate numerous and diverse findings to apply the full power of statistical methods to the task. Thus it is not a technique, rather it is a perspective that uses many techniques of measurement and statistical analysis.

Glass et al. (1981) move beyond assessing the properties of studies to considering how the data can be integrated, given those properties. Even in their positivism, they give us hope for the analogy between meta-analysis and meta-ethnography. First, they denote meta-analysis as an "attitude" and "perspective," reinforcing the idea that the concept is not limited to statistical applications. Second, they promote some humility, saying it is "nothing more than the attitude." They suggest that the concept, while important, is not a paradigm shift, but rather an elaboration of existing understandings about data analysis.

Hunter et al. (1982) elaborate Glass's general approach of "averaging results across studies" (p. 11). While they continue to include only quantitative studies, they highlight the essentially interpretive nature of meta-analysis. They argue, for example, that "restriction of scope should be topical rather than methodological" (p. 166). Further, they point to the inductive nature of all synthesis activities in arguing against exclusion of studies with "methodological deficiencies since 'deficiency' is usually based on a theory that is itself not empirically tested" (p. 186). The worth of studies, in their view and in ours, is determined in the process of achieving a synthesis.

As valuable as meta-analysis and integrative research reviews are as extensions of positivism, the synthesis enterprise itself is essentially an interpretive endeavor. As Ward (1983) argues: "'synthesis' can be used to refer to all efforts to relate knowledge, including previously unrelated or contradictory knowledge, and to show it is relevant to a specific situation or topic" (p. 26). Certainly, the accumulation of data may proceed by positivistic assumptions. Nonetheless, relating knowledge and showing its relevance is establishing its meaning: It is an interpretation (see Strike and Posner, 1983a).

Strike and Posner (1983b) extend the definition of synthesis along this line. They argue that:

> synthesis is usually held to be activity or the product of activity where some set of parts is combined or integrated into a whole. . . . [Synthesis] involves some degree of conceptual innovation, or employment of concepts not found in the characterization of the parts as means of creating the whole [p. 346].

Knowledge syntheses, to Strike and Posner, may take a number of forms. All forms are inductive: Based on the evidence, some interpretation is proposed. Further, these interpretations are judged by three criteria: whether they "clarify and resolve, rather than observe, inconsistencies or tensions between material synthesized"; whether a "progressive problem shift results"; and "whether or not the synthesis is consistent, parsimonious, elegant, fruitful, and useful" (Strike and Posner, 1983b: 356-357).

These criteria are all essentially interpretive, inquiring about the quality of the interpretation of various studies. It is indeed curious that, although the synthesis of knowledge has been conceived of as inductive and interpretive, the most-developed approaches are inductive and positivistic. As Mills (1959) suggests, this may be the result of an "abstracted empiricism" that relies on quantification more than on the testing of theoretically deduced hypotheses. The approach we call meta-ethnography is an attempt to develop an *inductive and interpretive* form of knowledge synthesis.

Synthesizing Understanding

We assert that the business of synthesis is essentially interpretive and inductive. However, no one has developed a description of what this interpretive synthesis involves. We believe it involves understanding the nature of interpretive explanation. As Spicer (1976: 341) writes:

> In the study there should be use of the emic approach, that is, the gathering of data on attitudes and values orientations and social relations directly from people engaged in the making of a given policy and those on whom the policy impinges. It should be holistic, that is, include placement of the policy decision in the context of the competing or cooperating interests, with their value orientations, out of which the policy formulation emerged; this requires relating it to the economic, political, and other contexts identifiable as relevant in the sociocultural system. It should include historical study, that is, some diachronic acquaintance with the policy and policies giving rise to it. Finally, it should include consideration of conceivable alternatives and of how other varieties of this class of policy have been applied with what results, in short, comparative understanding.

Qualitative research focuses on "meaning in context" (Mishler, 1979) and thus captures a uniqueness that more deductive approaches cannot. Meta-analysis and integrative reviews, as quantitative approaches, require a determination of a basic comparability between phenomena so that the data can be aggregated for the analysis. This is the crux of the problem with a meta-analysis analogy for a meta-ethnography. As will be seen in the failed synthesis of the desegregation ethnographies, the assumption of comparability stripped these studies of their interpretive merit and worth (Lincoln and Guba, 1980). Comparison became aggregating; holism became analysis; etic (the imposition of an outside frame of reference) became preferred over emic; and history became confounding.

Interpretive explanation does not yield knowledge in the same sense as quantitative explanation. Taylor (1982: 153) argues that interpretation in qualitative research "is an attempt to make clear, to make sense of an object of study. . . . The interpretation aims to bring to light an underlying coherence of sense." Schlechty and Noblit (1982) conclude that an interpretation may take one of three forms: (1) making the obvious obvious, (2) making the obvious dubious, and (3) making the hidden obvious. An interpretation that makes the "obvious obvious" is

Geertz's (1973) study of the Bali cockfight, in which the meaning of the games, Geertz found, was essentially an expression of the culture and had no other function. Bossert's (1979) study of task organization in classrooms revealed that the obvious explanation that differences in classrooms are due to differences in individual characteristics of teachers was dubious; differences in task organization was a better explanation. Everhart's (1983) interpretation of student culture reveals the hidden meaning of schooling and of resistance to schooling in terms of social reproduction of society; he makes the hidden obvious. Each of these studies makes clear both what the "sense of things" was and what implications that sense of things has for the human discourse.

Interpretive explanations are narratives through which the meanings of social phenomena are revealed. They represent the "multiperspectival reality" (Douglas, 1976) of any social event and the holistic meaning of these multiple perspectives. They teach an understanding of the meaning of a particular event in dialogue with a more universal audience (Schlechty and Noblit, 1982). They enable us not to predict but to "anticipate" (Geertz, 1973) what might be involved in analogous situations; they help us understand how things might connect and interact. An interpretation enables the reader to translate the case studied into his or her own social understanding: Interpretive accounts, above all, provide a perspective and, in doing so, achieve the goal of enhancing human discourse.

To appropriately synthesize understanding from qualitative studies, we must hold to the essential task of synthesis using both induction and interpretation. The nature of interpretive explanation is such that we need to construct an alternative to the aggregative theory of synthesis entailed in integrative research reviews and meta-analysis and be explicit about it. The influence of positivistic thinking is pervasive, yet subtle. An example will reveal how subtle and how dramatic this influence can be.

Not Seeing the Forest for the Trees: The Failure of Synthesis for the Desegregation Ethnographies

In 1975, the National Institute of Education (NIE) awarded six contracts for ethnographic field studies of urban desegregated schools. The decision to make the awards was controversial. However, in the end, Ray Rist was able to convince other NIE officials that such studies were appropriate to inform the research agenda of the newly formed Desegregation Studies Team. For NIE, studies that focused on the process of interracial schooling promised to generate new insights. The resulting studies accomplished this objective. Later, Rist (1979: 7) was to write:

> Despite the pressing need to learn more of the political and social dynamics of school desegregation, of the interactions within multiracial student populations, and of how schools learn to cope with new discipline and community relations matters, the research has been extremely limited. The very large majority of studies have not been grounded in the analysis of the day-to-day working out of school desegregation.

Almost three years later, detailed analyses of the schools were submitted to NIE, and NIE reviewers dubbed them successful studies but "gloomy" in terms of the outlook for school desegregation. The schools studied had initially been chosen because they were reputed to be good examples of desegregated schools within their respective school districts. The research teams found that, even in these "good" schools, desegregation was not smoothly implemented and had encountered significant resistance on many fronts. The schools even had considerable difficulty in defining the appropriate meaning of desegregation. Further, in the absence of such agreement, "business as usual" (Sagar and Schofield, 1979) was the reaction of schools. As a result, resegregation of the schools and classrooms ensued; order became a heightened priority; and the individual students, teachers, and administrators were left to fend for themselves (Rosenbaum, 1979).

The ethnographies, of course, revealed this more complexly than the above statement reveals. Interestingly, they raised for NIE and the researchers the problem of how to reduce the detailed site-specific findings into a set of results that could be communicated to policymakers. In the end, two rather different approaches were attempted under the guidance of Murray Wax. One approach was to summarize the similar lessons from all sites (Wax, 1979a) by condensing the five final reports submitted (one contractor did not submit a final report in time to be included). This approach was criticized by LeCompte (1979) for not providing credible and convincing support for the conclusions, due to lack of detail. Additionally, she argued, it ignored the idiosyncratic differences that seemingly were also policy-relevant.

The second approach was to ask the research teams to agree on a set of salient issues and conduct cross-site analyses based on the data from all the sites. This attempt did not include a set of commissioned critiques, as did the other attempt, but only a summary by Rosenbaum, an independent analyst (Wax, 1979b). (The above summary of the results is drawn from that attempt.)

Nevertheless, in large part, LeCompte's critique applies to the cross-site essays as well as to the final summary of the reports. She, we think, reasonably argued:

> The Wax summary of five ethnographic studies of desegregated schools promised a great deal but does not deliver as much as it promises. Both Practitioners and Academics reading such a document will be looking for answers—though of a different kind. Teachers, administrators, and politicians will be looking for guidelines and techniques that they can utilize toward the immediate solution of a pressing problem; academics will be hopeful of an explanation of the complex phenomena under examination, or at least a conceptual framework, consistently applied, which might explain variation in the phenomena. Neither are provided, although some useful insights can be teased out of the material presented. While it is difficult to quarrel with the well-stated initial premise—that ethnography is a particularly useful tool for studying processes such as those involved in desegregation of schools, and is a technique that provides insights garnered by no other means—the brevity of the report has obviated the richness of data and explanatory detail that is the hallmark of good ethnography and permits its conclusions to be well-grounded. What remains are some rather trite and atheoretical explanations for the failure of schools really to desegregate—such as the absence of effective leadership from the principals—and an idiosyncratic view of the whole process of desegregation which ignores some of the more important structural aspects of the conflict inherent in such a situation. In short, the article under review earns plaudits for what it attempts to do and some serious criticisms for what it fails to do [LeCompte, 1979: 118].

As condemning as this critique is, we believe it is instructive; it proposed that the summary attempt ended up being neither truly ethnographic nor informative. The desegregation ethnographies and the various attempts to communicate their findings (Clement et al., 1978; Collins and Noblit, 1978; Ianni et al., 1978; Scherer and Slawski, 1978; Schofield and Sagar, 1978; Rist, 1979; Henderson, 1981) all were able to offer adequate analyses of each site. How do we, then, account for the failure of the attempts to achieve ethnographic synthesis?

The Problem of Ethnographic Synthesis

The summary attempts (Wax, 1979a, 1979b) were essentially similar in their focus on attaining "general" conclusions. Wax wrote of the cross-site essay attempts:

> At a meeting in November 1977, agreement was reached that the investigating teams should participate in a small venture toward achieving more general conclusions from the ethnographic specifics of the separate cases. Each team proposed or was assigned a particular topic or theme, with the notion that its members could secure relevant data concerning each of the other sites. Thus, instead of five final reports, each of which might have mentioned something about a topic such as the relationship of lower-class black students to the school, there would be a single essay integrating the findings about the alienation of such students from schools that were supposedly desegregated [Wax, 1979b: 1].

Wax also described the condensation summary, saying the following:

> The present work constitutes an attempt to summarize and integrate the major findings of those five final reports into a compass of about 30,000 words. The work was commissioned with the hope that the process of textual integration would serve to bring forward the common findings among the five investigators, while the shortened size would mean a wider audience than might be gained by any single report. Moreover, it was also hoped that the textual integration would lead to a deemphasis of the faults and virtues of the particular sites while focusing attention on the common problems entailed in desegregating the schools [Wax, 1979a: v].

The summary attempts were experimental in that two different approaches, the cross-site essays (Wax, 1979b) and the integration of the final reports (Wax, 1979a), were pursued. The experiment did not vary *how* to summarize, only *what* to summarize: Both aimed to isolate the common findings and deemphasize the uniqueness of each site. Thus the experiment in reality compared the essay summary format with the full report summary format, with both focused on seeking common findings. While neither is an unusual way to summarize findings, they both entail an unstated theory of social explanation that focuses on aggregate patterns of results. As such, these summaries are akin to positivism, although we did not understand that at that time.

One might ask what is wrong with this approach. There is little wrong, except that the aggregation we engaged in (1) avoided a full exploration of context, and (2) did not enable an explanatory synthesis.

Since the publication of the summary attempts, Stephen Turner (1980) has provided us with a "theory of social explanation" that enables us to better understand what went wrong and what might be done about it. Turner's formulation is based in Winch's (1958) thesis about the nature of a social science and is especially appropriate to ethnographic analysis. He builds upon Winch's thesis to propose a theory of social explanation based in comparative understanding rather than in aggregation of data.

The desegregation summary attempts seemingly belie the rudiments of an ethnographic approach by ignoring "meaning in context" (Mishler, 1979). As Rosenbaum (1979) concluded from the cross-site essays, desegregation did have many different meanings in the schools studied. In these, context became the *confounding* variable in the search for common findings. The logic of the summary attempts essentially placed aggregation above understanding and left us in the difficult situation of attempting to discount the effects of context. Only Sullivan (1979a) escaped this trap. By concentrating on community context and conducting a comparative analysis of the five sites, Sullivan was able to assess how context affected desegregation and vice versa. Unfortunately, Sullivan's attempt was so powerful in identifying the contextually distinct meanings of race and desegregation that it resulted in the decision to delete contextual descriptions from the other essays. This decision contributed to the overall failure of synthesis.

Sullivan's summary attempt is instructive in another way. His comparative analysis, much like Turner's (1980) proposal, is the keystone to ethnographic synthesis. Not only does it maintain context as a salient component of analysis; it also avoids the aggregate issue. That is, he did not make general conclusions: The aggregation of uniqueness was simply nonsensical.

The aggregation approach to ethnographic synthesis that we employed in the desegregation ethnographies was not merely context-stripping. It actually impeded explanation and thus negated a true interpretive synthesis. The aggregation across-context procedure only defined and set puzzles. Further, the focus on commonalities probably resulted in inadequate definitions of the puzzles themselves. Better puzzle definition would have allowed context as part of the explanation. It would have required an explanation that "translates" the practices and conditions of one school into practices and conditions of the other schools. In short, LeCompte's (1979) critique of the final reports' summary (also applicable to the cross-site summaries, except possibly Sullivan's) is apt. We failed to provide the explanation that academics and practitioners might have wished. As is common in research, the failure is attributable to the methodology employed. We simply did not consider an alternative theory of social explanation.

Success from Failure

The failure to achieve an adequate synthesis for the desegregation ethnographies was, of course, disheartening to all involved. As scholars, we initially took it as a personal failure. However, if we make the effort to learn from failure, knowledge advances as much through failure as through success. In this case, there is much to be learned. On the one hand, this should teach us that even experienced ethnographers can be lulled into violating their paradigm when faced with an unusual task. As ethnographers, we carefully guarded our research from paradigm violations when we faced the familiar tasks of intensive, grounded research. As experienced and confident researchers, we approached the synthesis attempts with little trepidation and great enthusiasm. As is now apparent, research synthesis, especially ethnographic synthesis, must be more sophisticated than we imagined. By not having an explicit theory of social explanation to undergird the synthesis, we inappropriately relied on an aggregate theory.

This example is a revealing critique of the current state of ethnographic research. In general, we judge the quality of educational ethnography to be high. Nonetheless, the ethnographers' efforts to be grounded and empirical mean that we may eschew the more theoretical and philosophical issues that enable the paradigm to flourish and grow. If the paradigm seeks to create a knowledge base and inform practice, then we must find ways to synthesize our research. To regard these concerns as inappropriate and wrong thinking is a gross error. We can reduce our findings without being either overly reductionistic or falling prey to aggregate theories of synthesis. However, we must invest in the philosophy of our paradigm and elaborate alternative theories of social explanation to do so.

An alternative theory of social explanation that is appropriate to ethnography must be essentially interpretive. It must be both grounded and comparative. In the next chapter, we will use Turner's (1980) formulation of sociological explanation as translation. While our approach is comparative, we wish to dissociate our views from such anthropologists as Paul Shankman (1984). Shankman sees a comparative approach as enabling "generalizations" (p. 263). This is the essential flaw with the synthesis of the desegregation ethnographies. A comparative approach, to us, leads to *translations,* not generalizations. A meta-ethnography entails translating studies into one another.

The successes emerging from the failure of the desegregation synthesis attempts, then, are four. First, we have an awareness of the nature of the issue. Second, this awareness also revealed a direction in which to proceed. Third, this direction led to meta-ethnography as developed here. Finally, as we will show in Chapter 5, we are now able to provide a synthesis for the desegregation ethnographies.

Understanding and Knowledge

In the positivist paradigm, knowledge is thought to accumulate and thereby improve. The review of existing research is a prelude to deriving research questions and is used to justify the proposed research project as adding to the knowledge base. In qualitative research, we have a different view. First, we are not as concerned with knowledge (as a set of axiomatic "laws") as we are with understanding. Our research reveals that social life varies dramatically by context: Research is to help us understand how that occurs. As Geertz (1973) argues, the goal of qualitative research is to enrich human discourse, not to produce a formal body of knowledge. Second, while prior studies should, of course, inform proposed studies, a review of the literature in qualitative research is usually intended to establish the discourse to be addressed. However, in the process of studying something, interpretivists often discover a new area of discourse—that is, a new topic—to be enriched by their research. In doing so, an unanticipated understanding may develop that teaches us the limitations of the discourse we originally intended to inform. Third, qualitative researchers do not see accumulation as the vehicles with which to inform their sciences. The accumulation of studies merely indicates an arena of enduring human discourse. It may or may not reflect a substantive improvement in how well we understand something. Taking Kuhn's (1970) notion of "normal science" as being work done with a paradigm, qualitative researchers may argue that an accumulation of studies is a technical endeavor of simply playing out the paradigm or theory rather than any real advancement. Finally, positivists see accumulation of knowledge as a means to develop predictions. That is to say, once we have enough knowledge, the world will be predictable, if not controllable. Qualitative researchers, informed by the sociology of knowledge (Mannheim, 1936; Berger and Luckmann, 1967), see social life and culture as emergent. Knowledge, as accumulated culture, is always limited in its ability to predict since humans are reflective and use knowledge bases to create new social and cultural forms. By understanding the sense of things, anticipation, rather than prediction, is the more reasonable result of qualitative research.

One Basis for a Meta-Ethnography

One alternative to the aggregative theory is what we call meta-ethnography. We use this term, in part, because of the analogy to meta-analysis. We share the goal of those proposing meta-analytic and integrative research reviews of "putting together" all the research available to us. We hold to the "attitude" that Glass et al. (1981) suggest. Yet the analogy ends there. We use the phrase meta-ethnography to highlight our proposal as an interpretive alternative to research synthesis. For us, the *meta* in meta-ethnography means something different than it does in meta-analysis. It refers not to developing overarching generalizations but, rather, translations of qualitative studies into one another. This is a *meta*-ethnography in that it involves using the nature of interpretive explanation to guide the synthesis of ethnographies or other qualitative, interpretive studies.

We are the first to concede that our approach is but one of many possible approaches. The discourse about language and symbols in ethnographic research makes it inevitable that other approaches, also interpretive, will be discovered. As interpretivists ourselves, we look forward to the debate and the alternative perspectives. We acknowledge that our translation-based meta-ethnography is but *a* meta-ethnography.

A meta-ethnography involves some theory about how best to synthesize interpretive accounts. For this purpose, we have adapted Turner's (1980) notion that all explanation is essentially comparative and takes the form of translation. A meta-ethnography based in Turner's conceptualization simply extends his argument by constructing syntheses by translating multiple qualitative studies into one another's terms. In doing so, we must be careful to remember Turner's essential point: The analyst is always translating studies into his own world view. A meta-ethnography based in notions of translating studies into one another will inevitably be partially a product of the synthesizer. While positivists will be concerned, interpretivists will be less concerned. As Geertz (1973) argues, all ethnography is but interpretations of inter-pretations. The ethnographer is "inscribing" (p. 19) the cultural interpretations that others create and, in doing so, creates a reading of a culture. A meta-ethnography is but one more interpretation and largely takes the same form. In fact, we propose that it is best to treat all interpretive accounts, as well as the synthesis, as metaphoric: It was "as if" we failed to achieve a synthesis of desegregation ethnographies, even though we accumulated data, wrote reports, and made cross-site generalizations.

A meta-ethnography based in translating studies into one another obviously does not yield the same type of product as do meta-analysis and integrative research review. Translation can be an elaborate endeavor. Meta-analysis has been critiqued for overly long syntheses (Cahen, 1980). This problem may be endemic to synthesis attempts in general. However, we demonstrate that meta-ethnographic syntheses of small numbers of studies need not be overly long. The product, the translation of studies into one another, enables readers to simultaneously understand how the studies are related. Some studies may be appropriately characterized in the terms of other studies; others may not be. In this latter case, the translation reveals how different the interpretations are. These differences become a substantive part of the synthesis. Reciprocal translations of studies into one another enable holistic accounts that, according to Spicer's criteria for an ethnographic approach, are comparative, emic, and historical.

2. A META-ETHNOGRAPHIC APPROACH

A meta-ethnography starts, like all inquiries, with an interest in some setting, topic, argument, issue, controversy, or opportunity. This interest, for interpretivists, need not be overly specific. Often it starts simply from seeing what different qualitative researchers have to say about something and being concerned with how to compare their accounts. As one pursues this interest by reading qualitative studies, what is of interest undoubtedly changes. It may be modified, specified, or elaborated as one discovers new accounts. Our comparisons of studies are usually the most problematic aspect of this research process.

Once we have a general topic and a set of accounts that seemingly pertain to the topic, we begin systematic comparisons. A meta-ethnographic approach is one form of systematic comparison; it involves the translation of studies into each other. The collection of the translations constitutes a meta-ethnographic synthesis. We believe doing a meta-ethnography is best thought of as a series of phases that overlap and repeat as the synthesis proceeds.

Phase 1: Getting started. This involves identifying an intellectual interest that qualitative research might inform. As Yin (1984) suggests, qualitative approaches "are the preferred strategy when 'how' or 'why' questions are being posed, when the investigator has little control over events, and when the focus is on a contemporary phenomenon within some real-life context" (p. 13). An intellectual interest is immediately tempered and given form by reading interpretive accounts. In this phase, the investigator is asking, How can I inform my intellectual interest by examining some set of studies? In part, this phase is finding something that is worthy of the synthesis effort. This concern does not go away as the synthesis proceeds, as intellectual interest becomes elaborated and studies read. However, usually what is worthy about the synthesis effort will change. Following Patton (1980), a synthesis not worth doing is not worth doing well. There is no value in a synthesis that is not of interest to the author.

Phase 2: Deciding what is relevant to the initial interest. In meta-analysis and integrative research reviews, considerable effort is expended in developing an exhaustive list of studies that might be included. For interpretivists, such a decision needs some justification. If the intent is to synthesize *all* the ethnographies concerning island peoples, there must be some justifiable reason that such a synthesis makes sense. What can we learn from translating all island cultures into one another? The answer to this question seems to dictate gross generalizations that an interpretive meta-ethnography would find unacceptable. In a meta-ethnography, the translations interpretations can be generalized, but the simple accumulation of similarities and differences between cultural settings proves fruitless.

Deciding what studies or accounts are relevant involves knowing who the audience for the synthesis is, what is credible and interesting to them, what accounts are available to address the audiences' interests, and what your interests are in the effort. Certainly, it makes sense to be exhaustive in the search for relevant accounts when one's interest is not in the synthesis of specified, particular studies. Of course, as Cooper (1984), Hunter et al. (1982), and Light (1980) indicate, it is sometimes difficult to know when one is being exhaustive, given that not all studies are published and/or publicly available.

Hunter et al. (1982) provide a review of the abstracting services for studies, monographs, and articles. Ethnographic research in particular is likely to be in monograph or book form. Thus searches require use of standard library card catalogs, review of references at the end of related works, and probably discussions with scholars working in the general area. In the end, a meta-ethnography is driven by some substantive interest derived from comparison of any given set of studies. Studies of particular settings should always be regarded as particular. Unless there is some substantive reason for an exhaustive search, generalizing from all studies of a particular setting yields trite conclusions.

Phase 3: Reading the studies. Most proposed methods for research synthesis move quickly to analyzing the characteristics of the study relevant to the topic of interest. In qualitative research, the synthesis is more dynamic and develops throughout the synthesis effort. Therefore, in a meta-ethnography, this phase is not so clear. Rather, we think it is best to identify this phase as the repeated reading of the accounts and the noting of interpretative metaphors. Meta-ethnography is the synthesis of texts; this requires extensive attention to the details in the accounts, and what they tell you about your substantive concerns.

Phase 4: Determining how the studies are related. In doing a synthesis, the various studies must be "put together." This requires determining the relationships between the studies to be synthesized. We think it makes sense to create a list of the key metaphors, phrases, ideas, and/or concepts (and their relations) used in each account and to juxtapose them. Near the end of phase 4, an initial assumption about the relationship between studies can be made. Three different assumptions and illustrations of subsequent syntheses are developed in Chapters 3, 4, and 5.

Phase 5: Translating the studies into one another. In its simplest form, translation involves treating the accounts as analogies: One program is like another except. . . . On the other hand, translation is more involved than an analogy. Translations are especially unique syntheses, because they protect the particular, respect holism, and enable comparison. An adequate translation maintains the central metaphors and/or concepts of each account *in their relation to other key metaphors or concepts* in that account. It also compares both the metaphors or concepts and their interactions in one account with the metaphors or concepts and their interactions in the other accounts. We discuss this process in the next section of this chapter.

Phase 6: Synthesizing translations. Synthesis refers to making a whole into something more than the parts alone imply. The translations as a set are one level of meta-ethnographic synthesis. However, when the number of studies is large and the resultant translations numerous, the various translations can be compared with one another to determine if there are types of translations or if some metaphors and/or concepts are able to encompass those of other accounts. In these cases, a second level of synthesis is possible, analyzing types of competing interpretations and translating them into each other.

Phase 7: Expressing the synthesis. The existing literature on research synthesis is biased toward the written word. While it is no doubt true that most syntheses are written for an academic audience, the written synthesis is only one possible form. When the synthesis is driven by some concern to inform practitioners, other forms may be preferable. The audience itself may be employed to make the translations and to create symbolic forms appropriate to it. Videos, plays, art, and music all seem to be reasonable forms, depending on the audience and the form they respect (Patton, 1980).

While meta-ethnographic syntheses may be conducted by individuals solely for themselves, any effort to communicate the synthesis involves some assessment of the audience. To be effectively communicated, the synthesis must not only be in appropriate form but must also use intelligible concepts. Every audience has a language. For the translations of studies to achieve a synthesis, the translations must be rendered in the audience's particular language.

The intention here is not to pander to the audience. Having our syntheses readily intelligible does not mean reducing the lessons of ethnographic research to an everyday or naive understanding of a culture. The focus on translations is for the purpose of enabling an audience to stretch and see the phenomena in terms of others' interpretations and perspectives. To do this means we must understand the audience's culture in much the same way as we understand the studies to be synthesized; we must represent one to the other in both their commonality and their uniqueness. This is Turner's basic argument about sociological explanations as translations. The problems of getting the synthesis to the audience are discussed in further detail in chapter 6.

These, then, are the phases of conducting a meta-ethnographic synthesis. In practice, the phases overlap and may be parallel. Our substantive interests and our translations develop simultaneously. The synthesis is affected by its intended expression. Often, audience needs drive the form and substance of the synthesis. What is unique about a meta-ethnography, however, is not these phases, but the translation theory of social explanation that it involves. In the next section, we explore this theory of social explanation in more detail.

An Alternative Theory of Social Explanation

The methodological discussions of ethnography in educational research often define it as an "alternative" approach (Patton, 1975;

Noblit, 1981). A meta-ethnography certainly seems to imply an alternative theory of social explanation. It is often difficult to imagine what a reasonable alternative to synthesis as aggregation could be. As noted, Turner (1980) explored the issue of social explanation and suggests some directions. His work is of interest here because, as we will show, Turner's analysis establishes a theory of social explanation that can be extended to undergird a meta-ethnography, avoiding the problems we witnessed with the desegregation ethnographies.

Of course, Turner sought a theory of social explanation for all of social science—positivistic, interpretive, and critical—and, as such, he did not primarily direct his work toward the advancement of ethnography. Nevertheless, the three basic elements of his argument are consistent with an interpretive paradigm and an ethnographic approach. First, Turner argues that all social explanation is essentially comparative, implicitly or explicitly. Experimental designs, of course, are explicitly comparative; it is also true that single case studies are, at their base, comparative in the sense that the researcher uses his or her experience, knowledge, and/or expectations to discern what is of interest in the case (see Gouldner, 1970). As Turner (1980) writes:

> We proceed as though we hypothesized that where we should follow such and such rule, the members of another social group or persons in another social context would do the same [p. 97].

That is, researchers implicitly or explicitly use a "same practices hypothesis" (p. 97) in research. We can, of course, expand this notion and allow for more sophistication on the part of researchers. We argue that researchers may proceed by hypothesizing that what is of interest is that which varies from their own experience, knowledge, and expectations (i.e., a "different practices hypothesis").

Second, Turner claims that the breakdown of a "same practices hypothesis" (or a different practices hypothesis) yields an explanatory "puzzle." The puzzle seeks to explain why the practice differs from that explicitly or implicitly expected. The answer for Turner must be interpretive, citing different social and historical contexts, and differing values, norms, and/or social relations, as reasons. He is careful to show that statistical analyses are of limited utility in this process:

> Analysis of aggregate patterns can help set puzzles, and differences in aggregate patterns may require explanations that cite differences in

practices. But the question "why the different practice?" is not touched by the analysis [Turner, 1980: 97].

While aggregate analyses can set puzzles, explanations that solve puzzles are based in "translation" of one case into another. In the case of an implicit comparison, we see that value explicitness on the part of the researcher is vital for this "translation" to be effected. Turner sees "translation" as having the general form of an analogy: "the different practice in a social group or social context that raises puzzles is explained in a way that a different rule of a game is explained" (p. 97). In other words, he argues that we solve the interpretive puzzle (that raised by the observation of similar or differing social practices in interpretive accounts) by explaining how the observed social practice is alike and different from our own. We translate the observed practice into our practices by treating each as an analogy of the other. Thus it is impossible to synthesize ethnographic research by focusing on empirical observations themselves, as in a meta-analysis. We must focus on the translations.

It is important to consider the form of translation that Turner is proposing here. An analogy is not literal; rather, it conveys the sense of things. In semantics, translations can be either literal (word-for-word) or idiomatic (translating the meaning of the text) (Barnwell, 1980). An interpretive meta-ethnography would require the latter. The idiomatic translation of accounts into one another is the interpretive synthesis of these accounts. As with other types of translation, translations of studies will vary with the translators and we should argue about what makes better or worse translations.

Third, and finally, Turner argues that social explanation must be inductive and framed in terms of the comparison of cases that give rise to the puzzles. He writes:

> What is logically peculiar about . . . the question [concerning the necessity for a general framework in advance of the research] is that it seems to rest on the idea that "what is important" can be decided in advance of explanation or apart from it. It is illicit to prejudge the question of which facts about society are truly "fundamental.". . . Assessments of what is fundamental, if they are ever intelligible as factual claims, must be based on factual, valid explanation, and not vice versa [Turner, 1980: 77].

Each researcher will have different substantive interests, see different comparative puzzles, and achieve different syntheses.

Turner's theory of social explanation, even though proposed for all of social science, is especially helpful in our quest for a theory of social explanation that will guide a meta-ethnography. It is evident that his argument is paradigmatically appropriate for ethnography. Spicer's (1976) criteria for an ethnographic approach, quoted earlier, are subsumed in Turner's argument. Turner gives new impetus for Spicer's concern that ethnography be comparative. Spicer's criteria of holism and history are preserved under Turner's notion of translation of one case into the other. For Turner, it is the explanation that brings the holism and history into social research. Finally, Spicer's "emic" criteria is mirrored in Turner's last point, that explanation must be based on what is studied, rather than on a framework decided in advance.

Not only is Turner's argument paradigmatically appropriate for a meta-ethnography, it also constitutes a methodology for the synthesis of ethnographies. First, it reveals that the "data" of synthesis are interpretations and explanations rather than the data collected through interviews and observations. Second, it shows us that in the same way that interpretation is a comparative translation, synthesis is the translation of interpretations. A meta-ethnography appropriately proceeds by translating the interpretations of one study into the interpretations of another. Finally, Turner's analysis gives us the basic form of the translation itself: an analogy.

We should be cautious, of course, in extending Turner's theory of social explanation into an area that he was not addressing directly, and in specifying it as method. Such extension and specification can lead to inappropriate conclusions. Although we hope that others will critically consider what we have proposed thus far and offer alternatives, we are aware of one issue that is especially problematic. That is, as we move from translation of the data of cases to the translation of interpretations of cases, we change levels of abstraction. Nonetheless, it is not the case that a meta-ethnography is necessarily more "abstract" than a meta-analysis. Rather, it is that the abstractions of a meta-analysis, which are issues of theory and measurement, come early in the process. Since they yield numeric values, the technical meta-analysis is deceivingly "concrete." Conversely, consistent with the interpretive paradigm, a meta-ethnography is based in "grounded" explanations. It struggles to keep the issues involved in explanation conscious to the researcher and reader. At the same time, the explanations are themselves being translated into one another. Thus the technical meta-ethnography is deceivingly less "concrete" than a meta-analysis.

The key issue here is the nature of the interpretations. Since interpretations come in the form of narratives, we must be concerned about issues of language and knowledge. Language may be seen as an expression that attempts to communicate to others; knowledge may be seen as what we know or think we know. When knowledge is communicated to others, it must be expressed in ways that the others can understand: The process of communicating knowledge is one of translating symbol systems between two or more parties. In short, interpretation, as a form of communicated knowledge, is symbolic and thus metaphoric. As Brown (1977: 77) argues: "In the broadest sense, metaphor is seeing something from the viewpoint of something else, which means . . . that all knowledge is metaphoric." Brown's extreme stance, that is, that knowledge is essentially metaphoric, may be objectionable to all but those highly committed to an interpretive paradigm. It is reasonable to argue that grounded explanations of any ethnography may or may not be essentially metaphoric. However, abstractions from grounded explanations must be. That is, by treating these abstractions as metaphoric, we prevent premature closure on their meaning (Goetz and LeCompte, 1984). Certainly, all generalizations pay the price of empirical accuracy to any particular case, but a metaphoric explanation maintains the complexity of the case, while at the same time facilitating reduction of the data. Further, it is common practice for ethnographers to use metaphors as organizers for their explanations (Miles and Huberman, 1984). Thus a meta-ethnography is likely to involve translating metaphors of one interpretation into another. The abstraction in a meta-ethnography seemingly requires that the synthesis will involve and employ metaphors, since metaphors are involved in "the fundamental questions of similarity, identity, and difference" (Brown, 1977: 79).

Metaphors and Meta-Ethnography

Critics of the interpretive paradigm often argue against its relativism. Positivists generally believe that some things are better than others, and that there is a singular truth that can be ascertained. They seemingly lose all reason when faced with a paradigm that reveals the "multiperspectival realities" of social endeavors (Douglas, 1976). However, the relativism that positivists portray as a "straw" relativism. In practice, ethnographers rarely, if ever, find that "anything goes." Rather, different groups perceive differently and act differently. The interactions of all this make for some interesting, if often ironic, developments. Nonetheless, the range of perceptions observed is always limited by context and socialization. Thus the ethnographer reveals a limited relativism. Ethnographers can argue for and against conduct in terms of cultural appropriateness, vested interests, and desired end-states, even if they do not see prediction of such end-states as a reasonable endeavor (Geertz, 1984). No doubt, the discussion thus far of translations, analogies, and metaphors does little to reassure those who fear an extreme relativism that it is indeed possible to achieve a meta-ethnography with some criteria for what constitutes a good synthesis.

Fortunately, Brown (1977), Martin (1975), and House (1979) all consider this issue. Brown argues that there are three basic criteria for the adequacy of metaphors in social science: economy, cogency, and range. Economy is similar to the classic criterion of parsimony in theory. Essentially, a metaphor is adequate when it is the simplest concept that accounts for the phenomena and has a superior "ease of representation and manipulation" (p. 104). Cogency refers to an "elegantly efficient integration." A metaphor is adequate on this criteria when it achieves the explanation without "redundancy, ambiguity, and contradiction" (p. 104). Range refers to the "power of incorporating other symbolic domains" (p. 105), and metaphors can be assessed as to superiority of this "power." Martin suggests an additional criterion: apparency. He writes, "this ability of language to (seemingly) 'show' us experience rather than merely 'refer' to it—I shall term 'apparency'" (p. 168). For Martin, an adequate metaphor is one that is successful in "the making apparent of connotations" (p. 208). Finally, House, in his consideration of the "aesthetics" of evaluations, suggests "credibility" as a fifth criterion. That is to say, while adequate metaphors for research are consciously "as if" and involve a transference between a literal sense and an absurd sense of a word or phrase (Brown, 1977), adequate metaphors also must be credible to, and understood by, the audience of the study.

In a meta-ethnography, the metaphors employed in the studies to be synthesized are assessed by these criteria and a determination made as to whether the emic metaphors are adequate to synthesize diverse studies. Further, if new metaphors are necessary to accomplish the synthesis, then alternative metaphors and sets of metaphors similarly are considered and judged. A meta-ethnography, then, treats interpretations as metaphors to effect the comparative translation of one study into others. The adequacy of the metaphors, and thus the meta-ethnography, is assessed by these five criteria.

The Judgment Calls

Richard Light (1980) discusses what he believes are the key judgment calls to be made in quantitative research syntheses. He argues that the "art" of synthesis involves the analyst's judgments at key decision points. The judgment calls in quantitative research synthesis are inclusion (which studies should be included), summary measures to be used, reliability of variables across studies, and the attitude brought to the judgments about the basic character of that being studied. Interpretivists likely see this list of judgment calls as clearly insufficient; they point to key decisions regarding what is of interest, how to compare, interpret, and synthesize, and so on. Thus a meta-ethnography is perhaps better understood not as key decision points, but as an ongoing process. Substantive interests and the studies relevant to the interests develop and change throughout a meta-ethnographic synthesis. Our translations are emergent and interactive as we search for adequate metaphors to express the studies and their relationships. Our syntheses are always merely a "reading" (Geertz, 1973). By experimenting with different readings, we further develop our metaphors, translations, and syntheses.

This is not meant to imply, however, that judgment calls are any less crucial to the art of qualitative research synthesis than they are to the art of quantitative synthesis. Rather, in qualitative research, the values of the researcher are ubiquitous. Typically, the issue of judgment calls in qualitative research is dealt with not as a problem, but as a necessary part of the interpretation. As Geertz (1973) argues, the ethnographer is akin to an inscriber; we inscribe our interpretation upon a culture. Thus each interpretation is both of the culture studied and of the ethnographer. In a meta-ethnography, this issue has one more level. Each account to be synthesized is already an interpretation of interpretations (Geertz, 1973). The translations of accounts raises this to another level: interpretations of interpretations of interpretations. The person conducting the synthesis is intimately involved in the synthesis that results.

In qualitative research, the issue of judgments and biases is accepted and included in the account created. The values and experiences of the interpreter are made explicit and often are intricately woven into the account. On the level of a meta-ethnography, the synthesizer must also be value-explicit and weave these into the syntheses. Similarly, the synthesis itself should be viewed as an interpretation and, as such, subject to critique and debate. Since an enriched human discourse is the goal of interpretivism, the nature of the debate, and not the synthesis itself, should be regarded as evidence of the success of a meta-ethnography. A judgment call of primary interest to the qualitative researcher is the assessment made by the audience of the worth of the account.

There are, of course, a number of technical decisions to be made as part of a meta-ethnography. Thankfully, most of these decisions are strategic (see Patton, 1980) and purposive. You develop an initial strategy and employ it until that strategy yields something substantive that you wish to pursue more purposively. The initial strategy of a meta-ethnography involves determining your assumptions about the synthesis effort. This, of course, is a means of being value explicit, revealing to your audience your initial assumptions about the nature of the synthesis. The initial strategy of reading the studies and reducing them metaphorically enables the synthesizer to tentatively decide how to treat the relationships between the studies. This decision may be revisited as the translations are made to show the adequacy of the initial assumptions.

Certainly, any set of studies may be related to each other in many ways. However, for the purposes of conducting a meta-ethnography, the key assumption is one of three possibilities: (1) the accounts are directly comparable as "reciprocal" translations, (2) the accounts stand in relative opposition to each other and are essentially "refutational," or (3) the studies taken together represent a "line of argument" rather than a reciprocal or refutational translation. Once the initial strategy yields a tentative assumption about the relationships *between* the studies, the next strategy is to construct translations based on this assumption. The assumption of a reciprocal translation can be discredited if the translations reveal opposition. In essence, the assumption of a reciprocal translation is dubious when the analogy between the studies fails. The assumption of a refutational translation fails when what initially appears to be opposition is revealed to be either directly analogous or about topics so different that some framework (i.e., a line of argument) is needed to make a synthesis possible. A line-of-argument assumption is not reasonable when the studies are revealed to be either directly analogous or oppositional.

A meta-ethnographic synthesis is complete when the assumptions have been checked, the appropriate translations made, a text created that reveals the process, and synthetic results reported in a form appropriate to some audience. The initially assumed and later determined relationship between the accounts, however, dramatically affects the nature of the translations. The nature of the different types of translations is the subject of the next part of this book.

Conclusion

Part I provides an introduction to the idea of a meta-ethnography and one approach to a meta-ethnography. Synthesizing understanding from qualitative studies requires a different theory of synthesis than that being employed in integrative research reviews and meta-analysis. We propose a translation theory of synthesis that entails the reciprocal translations of key metaphors or concepts employed in the accounts to be synthesized.

The process of conducting a meta-ethnographic synthesis involves many of the same aspects as any knowledge synthesis effort. Reading the studies and identifying the key metaphors enables an initial puzzle about the relationship between the studies of interest. This puzzle allows translations to begin. In the process of preparing an adequate translation, the initial puzzle is checked and, if found adequate, the synthesis is carried to completion. If not, other puzzles are made and checked until the appropriate puzzle and the appropriate translation is discovered.

A meta-ethnography requires that the appropriate theory of social explanation be essentially interpretive. For us, an interpretive explanation takes the form of a translation of one case into another, explicitly using an hypothesis of same or different social practices between the cases. This form of social explanation is essentially inductive and does not require a prior conceptual framework.

A meta-ethnographic synthesis is the synthesis of interpretive explanations that we take to be metaphoric in essence. This enables us to focus on the fact that all explanations are abstractions. Our goal is to represent, in a reduced form, the complexity revealed through the ethnography. It is only through metaphoric reductions that we can achieve both abstraction and complexity, and create translations that preserve the relations between concepts.

Part II

CONSTRUCTING META-ETHNOGRAPHIES

Syntheses usually involve "putting together" studies that are about similar things. Policymakers, students, and other audiences often wish to learn what is known about some specific topic, and thus proceed to collect the studies that address the specific topic. After collecting such studies, the next step is to determine how to put them together. For interpretivists, the appropriate synthesis should not be decided independent of the substance of the studies. As the studies are read, the points of similarity, overlap, or connection are discerned. Ethnographies may be related to each other in four ways: First, they can be about different things; second, they can be studies about roughly similar things; third, they can be studies that refute each other; and, fourth, they can be studies that successfully "build" a line of argument.

When ethnographies are about essentially different things, there is little reason to attempt to synthesize them. In Part II, we will discuss syntheses of studies that are about similar things, or refute each other, or suggest a line of argument. When ethnographies are about similar things, they can be synthesized as reciprocal translations of each study into the others. Creating reciprocal translations is the topic of Chapter 3. Some studies refute each other. Chapter 4 addresses refutational syntheses. Some set of studies suggest a line of argument, or inference, about some larger issue or phenomenon. Chapter 5 discusses this and presents an example. Once the appropriate synthesis has been attempted, the problem of how to express and inscribe the synthesis is evident. Chapter 6 discusses these issues of writing a meta-ethnography.

3. RECIPROCAL TRANSLATIONS AS SYNTHESES

As discussed earlier, we conceive of meta-ethnographic syntheses as translations (one case is like another, except that . . .). When ethnographies are roughly about similar things, the synthesis takes the form of reciprocal translations of each case into each of the other cases. That is to say, in an iterative fashion, each study is translated into the terms (metaphors) of the others and vice versa. When the studies can be

There are, of course, a number of technical decisions to be made as directly translated into another account, these reciprocal translations may reveal that the metaphors of one study are better than those of others representing both studies, or that some other set of metaphors, not drawn from the studies, seems reasonable. However, uniqueness of studies may not make it possible for a single set of metaphors to adequately express the studies. In these cases, we learn more from the translations than from the metaphors alone.

In reading ethnographic accounts, our focus needs to be on the concepts, themes, organizers, and/or metaphors that the authors employ to explain what is taking place. These are the things to translate across studies. This requires not only careful reading, but also attention to which metaphors, themes, concepts, or organizers enable us to fully render the account in a reduced form. This process is facilitated by the emerging conclusion about how the studies in question relate to each other. Once we know that the studies are similar and what metaphors the authors employ, we proceed to construct the "reciprocal" translations.

Two Examples

Our preceding discussion of meta-ethnography involving reciprocal translations can be concretized by some examples. The examples we use are drawn from the works of Wolcott (1973), Metz (1978), and Collins and Noblit (1978). For simplicity, we first synthesize Wolcott and then Metz with Collins and Noblit, and then engage in a limited assessment of the adequacy of the metaphors.

All syntheses begin with some interest on the part of the synthesizer. These two syntheses share the original interest in the phenomena of social order. They differ largely in that they are conducted with different foci. The school principal synthesis focuses on the role of the administrator in the social order of the school. We teach, in part, educational administration and have very practical interests in this topic (see Noblit and Johnston, 1982). The crisis of authority synthesis cuts across levels of analysis focusing on how belief systems interact, but also on the administrator's role in context. We write and teach in the areas of organizational theory and qualitative research. This synthesis enables a more holistic understanding of what schools are about. Both as teachers and as researchers, we are interested in what educational ethnography can teach us. Both of these syntheses enable us to systematically compare some of our own research to that of others. We better understand our own studies by translating them into other studies.

Our interests drive the meta-ethnographies that follow. They also have some effect on what we take to be the key metaphors and thus effect the translations themselves. We read the manuscripts repeatedly and chose these metaphors as basic to the account. Like all interpretations, a meta-ethnography is but a "reading" of what is studied. Other readings are possible and are to be encouraged. However, all interpretations must be grounded in the texts to be synthesized; the chosen metaphoric reductions are to be judged by their ability to portray the essence of these texts. Without such reductions, synthesis is not possible. The nature of the reductions, and the choices made, are reasonable topics of discussion and critique; additionally, of course, these contribute to the interpretivist goal of enlarging and enriching human discourse.

SCHOOL PRINCIPAL'S SYNTHESIS

Wolcott (1973) studied the principal of a suburban, middle-class elementary school in the Pacific Northwest and wrote what is now a classic study, *The Man in the Principal's Office*. Collins and Noblit (1978) studied the process of desegregation and interracial education in an urban, Southern, recently desegregated high school. In the course of the study, they happened to be witnesses to a natural experiment that resulted from the transfer of a principal and his replacement. Wolcott's study was largely descriptive; Collins and Noblit used the context and the principal's conduct to explain the form desegregation took in the school. It might be thought that these rather divergent studies would be difficult to synthesize. As we will show, they have a parallel set of metaphors, and the analyses can be seen as analogies, therefore making our meta-ethnography possible.

In Figure 3.1, we identify the major metaphors each study employs concerning the school principal. Each study seems to have three sets of metaphors central to the analysis: metaphors for the context, for the principal's conduct, and for the situation that was created. Since Wolcott's study was descriptive, it is important not to treat the situation metaphor as an "effect." As Wolcott explains, "maintaining the system" is more like an ongoing logic to the school and school district. It was this logic that socialized the principal and that the principal then promoted through his conduct. For Collins and Noblit, the situation metaphors are more like "effects." However, they also note that the situation resulted from a challenge (desegregation) to the normal logic of the

	Wolcott (1973)	Collins and Noblit (1978)	
Context:	"Freedom to make no serious mistakes" (p. 306)	"fishbowl" (p. 66) "threat and promise" (p. 81)	
Conduct:	"patience" (p. 296) "prudence" (p. 306)	(1st principal) "negotiated order" (p. 78)	(2nd principal) "bureaucratic order" (p. 78)
Situation:	"maintaining the system" (p. 227)	"stratification" (p. 150) "conflict" (p. 162)	"white flight" (p. 171) "closed" (p. 75)

Figure 3.1: Metaphors for School Principal's Synthesis

school district and school, and the interaction of that challenge with the conduct of the two principals.

For Wolcott's study, the context was one of a "freedom to make no serious mistakes" in the face of multiple constituencies and conflicting expectations about both the school and the principal's role. In such a context, the principal's conduct was a balance of the "patience" not to act precipitously and the "prudence" to recognize times in which action was necessary. Patience was engendered by the conflicting expectations for the role and the consequent uncertainty. Prudence was constrained similarly in that the opportunities to exert leadership were actually few, with the exception of resolving problems that emerged to threaten the "smooth" operation of the school. Since Wolcott's principal had conflicting expectations, could not act precipitously without jeopardy, and could not establish a new direction, the man in the principal's office was a cog in "maintaining the system."

For Collins and Noblit's study, the existent context was altered by desegregation, and thus was more problematic. Desegregation placed the school under increased scrutiny ("fishbowl") and constituted both "a threat and a promise." If desegregation went smoothly, reputations were to be made; if it did not, careers would be in jeopardy. It was "freedom to make no serious mistakes" in a politically charged, emotionally heated, and court-ordered innovation. The first principal, a black male, was transferred into a formerly all-white school that had served the wealthiest neighborhood in the city. The staff was desegregated at the same time. However, the remaining white staff and students had considerable influence in the district and the city. While the principal was committed to desegregation, he recognized the influence of these participants and set about creating a "negotiated order." The negotiations were heated and led to factionalization of the staff, and to a lesser extent, the students. The white staff and students coalesced, and thus had the power to negotiate. They negotiated for the white staff to teach college preparatory and advanced placement classes (which they, of course, had done for the rather elite student body before desegregation) as well as to select the eligible students for such courses. In the end, white students were largely instructed by white teachers in college preparatory courses; black students were taught by black teachers in general and remedial courses. Some desegregation was experienced in the courses that fell in the lower strata of college preparatory and the higher strata of general courses. Under "negotiated order," the school had "stratification" in its curriculum by race. The first principal attempted to challenge the power of the white teachers and students ("conflict"). But he lost—and was transferred—to be replaced by a second black male principal. This principal decided the school needed an order that was to emanate from his office. His "bureaucratic order" brooked no opposition and denied the power of existing social networks to define the situation. The school became unnervingly quiet and "closed." However, the white staff and students were denied their former power and status and responded by not accepting the authority of the principal. "White flight" from the school resulted. White teachers retired or transferred. Those who could not depart quickly performed ritualistically, as they sought opportunities to leave. White students left for private academies, moved residences to the county and attended county schools, and encouraged siblings and neighbors to do likewise. Under "bureaucratic order," desegregation resulted in the school's being identified as a "black" school.

The elaborations of the metaphors employed in the two ethnographies reveal that each set is seemingly adequate to summarize its case. Further, the parallels between the cases are legion, although each case is quite unlike the other in terms of region, level of school, population served, and desegregation. In fact, Noblit (1979) later concluded that "patience" and "prudence" were more apt metaphors than "negotiated order" and "bureaucratic order." Obviously, the "freedom to make no serious mistakes" metaphor is cogent to both, although the prospect of committing an error was heightened by desegregation.

The situation metaphors seem less able to be translated into one another. This is overcome, however, by elaborating the "maintaining the system" metaphor for the Collins and Noblit case. We argue that the political power of the whites was actually part and parcel of the "system": The city and district resisted desegregation and thus were chided by a federal judge for their "bad faith" in the implementation of desegregation. They were "maintaining the system." Given this argument, a full translation is achieved and a synthesis attained. It also appears that Wolcott's metaphors are more adequate for the synthesis than those of Collins and Noblit. They are more economical, cogent, cover the range between the studies, have an apparency (as the "maintaining the system" discussion reveals), and are at least as credible.

"CRISIS OF AUTHORITY" SYNTHESIS

Metz (1978), in *Classrooms and Corridors,* studied two junior high schools in a Northern urban area shortly after the schools were desegregated. As explained previously, Collins and Noblit studied one desegregated urban Southern high school. Metz was concerned with the "crisis of authority" in these schools and explained it in terms of a conflict between academic and order goals. Similarly, Collins and Noblit were concerned about a goal conflict, but between the goals of education and desegregation. Again, for this synthesis we use studies that are rather divergent, but nevertheless, amenable to synthesis under our scheme for a meta-ethnography.

In Figure 3.2, we identify the major metaphors each study employs concerning the crisis of authority. Each study seems to have four sets of metaphors central to the analysis: metaphors for teachers, students, principals, and effects. Both studies are analytic and focus on explaining the observed effects. However, it is unlikely that the authors, as ethnographers, see the analysis as a simple cause and effect chain.

For Metz's first school, the teachers were unified and had an "incorporative" ideology (teacher-centered). The students were stratified into curriculum tracks by compliance and race as well as ability. This stratification affected their beliefs and perceived roles in the school and classroom. The college preparatory track white students saw themselves as "junior partners" to the teachers in the educational process and actively participated in negotiating the teacher's role. The general studies track white students more readily accepted the school's right to define their roles than did the "junior partners." These students focused primarily on issues of "human decency and fairness." The black students had quite different beliefs. The college track blacks perceived racism in the curricula but they also "recognized the usefulness" of their access to the high track for later careers. The general track blacks,

	Metz (1978)		Collins and Noblit (1978)	
	(School 1)	(School 2)		
Teachers:	"incorporative" (p. 168)	"incorporative" (p. 168) "developmental" (p. 168)	"old guard" (p. 67) "new teachers" (p. 102)	
Students:	"junior partners" (p. 78) "human decency and fairness" (p. 81) "recognized the usefulness" (p. 83) "shut out" (p. 85)		"honor students" (p. 67) "active blacks" (p. 82) "freaks" (p. 85) "Red Oaks blacks" (p. 82)	
Classroom Order:	"principled conflict" (p. 125)		"two schools under one roof" (p. 84)	
			(1st principal)	(2nd principal)
	"order" (p. 189) "own responsibility ...first" (p. 189) "accepting opposition ...from no one" (p. 189)	"academic" (p. 189) "delegating" (p. 201) "mediated" (p. 201)	"negotiated order" (p. 78)	"bureaucratic order" (p. 78)
Effects:	"orderly" (p. 240) "failed to engage skeptical students" (p. 240)	"commitment" (p. 240) "disorder" (p. 240)	"stratification" (p. 150) "conflict" (p. 102)	"white flight" (p. 82) "closed" (p. 75)

Figure 3.2: Metaphors for Crisis of Authority Synthesis

believing they were "shut out" of all but remedial work, saw little reason to participate in the educational process. These belief systems usually interacted smoothly. But, "principled conflict" often occurred when teachers' and students' perceptions of each other's roles did not match, especially when teachers believed that their position alone should guarantee respect, deference, and obedience. The principal of this school focused on the "order" goal over the academic goal and saw his "own responsibility . . . first" as "accepting opposition . . . from no one." The net effect of the interaction of these belief systems was that they "kept a reasonably orderly, safe school, but one that failed to engage the skeptical students."

Metz's second school had a teaching staff that was divided between "incorporative" (teacher-centered) and "developmental" (child-centered) ideologies. The students, however, shared the stratification and general beliefs characterized in the first school. In general, developmental teachers engendered less principled conflict with students. Even so, classroom interaction was facilitated by teachers and students sharing the same perceptions of each other's roles, as in the first school. The principal perceived his role differently than the principal of the first school, possibly because of the teachers' ideological division. He admitted that there was conflict between the order and academic goals, but focused on the "academic" goal, and through "delegating," "mediated" the problems that emerged. As a result, the school "overcame some of the students' alienation, and won higher levels of commitment, but left itself open to significant disorder." There was such disorder, in fact, that the principal resigned under pressure.

Collins and Noblit's school had an observed split between "old guard" and "new teachers," who were, in Metz's terms, incorporative and developmental, respectively. The high school had basically four student networks. The "honor students" were white and generally took college preparatory and advanced placement courses with "old guard" teachers. The "freaks" were a racially mixed, but largely white, counterculture network. While "freaks" were found in a wide range of courses and levels of instruction, they normally populated the lower levels of the college preparatory courses and upper levels of the general courses. Thus they experienced both "old guard" and "new teachers." The "active blacks" were black students who were visible participants in school activities, student council, and the like. Only a few of these students were in courses with the "honor students." They shared the levels of instruction populated by the "freaks." Notably, unlike the "freaks," these students were committed to school and later careers. The "Red Oaks blacks" were a network of lower class students who lived in a public housing project and exclusively populated the remedial and lower level general courses.

Even in the politically charged atmosphere of this school, classroom interaction was generally smooth. In part, this was because the "old guard" taught the "honor students" and white students, as a rule, and the "new teachers" taught the others, including virtually all the black students. This stratification reinforced vested interests of both the students and the teachers, since each set of networks distrusted the other. "Two schools under one roof" prevailed. Each was orderly; overt conflict was avoided as long as each set of networks kept to itself. As discussed earlier, the two principals exemplified "negotiated order" and "bureaucratic order" in succession. The interaction of the networks under "negotiated order" promoted a stratification by race within the school, giving whites a more desirable status. Under "bureaucratic order," the school became "closed": Conflict was suppressed and staff and students retreated to the refuge of individual classrooms. However, desegregation as a goal was nullified, as the whites chose to leave the school rather than accept "bureaucratic order" and a loss in their power and status.

The elaborations of the metaphors employed in these two ethnographies reveal that each set is seemingly adequate to summarize its case. Further, it is apparent that school one (Metz) and "bureaucratic order" (Collins and Noblit) are essentially similar. School two (Metz) and "negotiated order" (Collins and Noblit) are also similar. Thus what would have been a comparison of four cases is summarized as an analogy between two. Further, we note the benefit of synthesizing cases that approach an ethnographic study differently. Collins and Noblit focused on social networks similar to social anthropologists; Metz focused on belief systems similar to cultural anthropologists. Thus, in the synthesis of these two perspectives, our meta-ethnography reveals that the established, white networks of staff had an incorporative ideology while the teachers transferred in had a developmental ideology. Student networks were similarly stratified by track, race, and social compliance in all the schools. The principals who chose order goals and enforced them, "traded off" commitment *to* the school for order *in* the school. Yet it is unclear whether this "singular focus" also overcame an ideological and political split among the staff. The principals who chose other goals (academics or desegregation), then mediated and negotiated to achieve decisions, "traded off" disorder (division among the staff) for commitment to the school. These studies cannot address what would happen in the latter case, since there were significant divisions among the staff in both studies. Wolcott's study, however, seems to suggest that without such divisions, a principal is likely to have a smoothly operating school and not be in jeopardy of losing the principalship. Finally, note that in both studies, students have power only when coalesced with staff, attesting to the "dependency" of their role.

In this synthesis, we find the metaphors of neither study more adequate. In part, this is because the different analytic focus used in each study is complementary, and thus one cannot be supplanted for the other. The language we use in the above synthesis contains new metaphors such as "division," "singular focus," "trade off," and "dependency." These metaphors have more adequate economy, cogency, range, apparency, and credibility for a meta-ethnographic synthesis than those of either study.

Conclusion

To illustrate a meta-ethnography based in reciprocal translations, we chose the cases of Wolcott, Metz, and Collins and Noblit. We show that the cases can be synthesized, and thus understood in terms of each other. For example, while Wolcott's case involves a suburban, middle-class Pacific Northwest elementary school and Collins and Noblit's case involves an urban, Southern, recently desegregated high school, both cases are rendered understandable through a meta-ethnographic synthesis. While Collins and Noblit studied high schools, and Metz studied junior high schools, it is apparent that our understanding of each study is enhanced by comparing and translating them.

Yet, as we noted, this type of synthesis requires the assumption that the studies can be "added" together. That is, they are clearly studies about some similar things. As we will discuss in the next chapter, when the assumption of similarity is not reasonable, a different approach is needed.

4. REFUTATIONAL SYNTHESIS

Kuhn (1970) has argued that science is not a simple accumulation of knowledge. Rather, science is marked by disagreements over paradigms that may result in paradigm revolutions. While social science does not necessarily follow the same patterns as the natural and physical sciences, it is evident that much research is geared not only to advance a perspective but also to refute other perspectives. Ethnographies that are implicitly or explicitly refutations of each other should not be synthesized in the form of reciprocal translations. Studies that have refutational agendas are amenable to the general meta-ethnographic approach developed in this book, but require a more elaborate set of translations—translations of both the ethnographic accounts and the refutations.

To be truly ethnographic, the synthesis must "take into account" the implied relationship between the competing explanations. The implied refutation, then, is analyzed substantively and subsequently incorporated into the synthesis. Our approach treats the refutation itself as part of the interpretation to be synthesized. In this way, we also can reduce it metaphorically and incorporate it into our translational approach to meta-ethnography.

When Ethnographies Don't Add, Analyze Refutations

Refutations are a specific form of interpretation. In one sense, a refutation is an interpretation designed to defeat another interpretation. In another sense, all interpretations have the form of a proposal about the way things are. To the extent that the interpretation claims to be reasonable, it implies a critique of other possible interpretations: an implied refutation. Implicit refutations, in some ways, are the most problematic in that they require a determination of the essential nature of the explanations, as well as whether reciprocal synthesis is possible. In the process of making this determination, we, in essence, transform an implied refutation into an explicit one. Once we make the refutations explicit, we may attempt a meta-ethnographic synthesis.

On the other hand, some interpretations are explicit about the nature of their refutation and are consciously structured to achieve that refutation. Explicit refutations have considerable potential for promoting reflectivity and enriching the human discourse. Explicit refutations are the enticing moments of intellectual discourse, exhibiting both our belief systems and our ways of arguing. They are explanations not of findings but of the significance of the findings. Even the popular media finds them of interest, as the Derek Freeman (1983) refutation of Margaret Mead attests. Refutations are phenomena that can be considered in their own right. They have social meaning independent of the studies upon which they are based and can be considered as explanations distinct from those of the ethnographic accounts. Conceived in this manner, refutations are amenable to meta-ethnographic synthesis. Refutations can be translated into other refutations in ways similar to the translations possible for ethnographic accounts. Further, they are also amenable to similar processes of metaphoric reduction, which then serve as the basis of translations for a meta-ethnographic synthesis.

Two examples demonstrate refutational syntheses. In the first example, our interest was captured by an exchange of comments in *Anthropology and Education Quarterly*. Having read and taught from the works of both authors, we knew that, while both authors termed their works ethnographic, they were about quite different things. In the second example, our interest was first captured by the popular media's attention to Derek Freeman's book. We wondered why this book was receiving so much attention.

The Everhart-Cusick Debate

In 1985, Robert Everhart (1985a, 1985b) and Philip Cusick (1985a, 1985b) each reviewed a recent work of the other in *Anthropology and Education Quarterly*. In the same issue, each commented on the other's review. Interestingly, each finds no fault with the other's account, but rather faults the interpretation of the account.

We chose this debate for a number of reasons. First, it is a debate in a primary forum for educational ethnography, *Anthropology and Education Quarterly*. Second, the debate seems to be one with implications for the basic theoretical schools of thought in ethnographic research, Marxism and functionalism. Third, the debate is extensive and explicit, allowing both point and counterpoint, a relatively rare completeness even among explicit refutations. In short, then, it is an ideal opportunity for a refutational meta-ethnographic synthesis.

A meta-ethnographic synthesis first entails identification of the major metaphors with which ethnographers construct their interpretations. These metaphors, then, are the basis of reducing the ethnography, making it amenable to translation and thus a meta-ethnographic synthesis. Therefore, our first step is to construct the metaphoric reduction of the ethnographies themselves so as to develop the basis of the subsequent refutation. The matrix in Figure 4.1 displays the major metaphors of each ethnography.

Everhart's (1983) study of student groups in junior high school reveals that schooling engenders resistance to itself and, furthermore, that this resistance reproduces schooling. Everhart's metaphors have two bases: critical theory and emic student beliefs. He argues that schools reproduce capitalism by the "proletarianization" of students through a structure of hierarchical authority, students as "empty vessels," and instruction as "passing out information." Everhart further claims that these schools place an emphasis on "reified knowledge" as the "commodity" to be exchanged, learning as "the right answer," and large group processing with "standardizing activities." This results in significant amounts of time spent on "organizational maintenance" and a "minimization" of the demand for student involvement in instruc-

	Everhart (1983)	Cusick (1983)
Context:	"proletarianization" (p.30)	"growth, industrialization, and movement" (p. 10) "positive knowledge" (p. 4)
Formal Structure:	"hierarchical authority" (p.1) "reified knowledge" (p.86) students as "empty vessels" (p.59) instruction as "passing out information" (p.38) learning as "the right answer" (p.59) "standardizing activities" (p.39)	"the egalitarian ideal" (p.1) "biracialism" (p. 13) "maintenance of public confidence" (p.3) "attendance and discipline" (p.25)
Substructure:	"organizational maintenance" (p. 236) "estranged" (p.88) students "void" (p.78) "waiting" (p.50) "regenerative knowledge" (p.124) "opposition" (p.127) "reappropriation" (p.192) "picking on students" (p.142) "making light of everything" (p.157) "goofing off" (p.165) "beating the system" (p.211) "jockey for position" (p.168) "contradiction" (p.109)	"keep the lid on" (p. 22) "open elective system" (p. 16)" teachers "free" to create curricula (p. 43) "get along with kids" (p. 34) "mutual liking" (p. 65) "entrepreneurial approach" (p. 66) "outside interests" (p. 99)

Figure 4.1: Metaphors for Ethnographic Synthesis

tional activity. The result is that students are "estranged" from their labor. They fill the structural "void" of "waiting" for instruction with the creation of social groups. The creation and maintenance of these social groups involves "regenerative knowledge," an interpretive knowledge system that stands in "opposition" to the reified knowledge of the school. This opposition is a "reappropriation" of student control. It takes the form of a "game," involving "picking on students," "making light of everything," "goofing off," "bugging the teacher" (through changing agendas, writing notes, being a pest, and humor), and "beating the system" (by smoking, cheating, and skipping school and classes). Further, these student groups "jockey for position" and consequently stratify the student population. Everhart critically analyzes this reappropriation, concluding that it contains a fundamental "contradiction." He argues that instead of critically opposing the structure of schooling, it serves as a "release," enabling schools to reproduce the labor process of a capitalist society.

It is apparent, then, that Everhart's interpretation has elements of (and metaphors for) contextual conditions, formal structure, and substructure (see Figure 4.1). Further, the interpretation is essentially dialectical in its emphasis on both opposition and contradictions.

Although Cusick's analysis is also structural, his (1983) study is rather different from Everhart's. First, his focus is on the school as created by staff, not students. Second, he wishes to construct an "abstracted model" of structure from studies of three high schools. That is, he searches for generalizability. While two of the schools are urban and biracial, one is suburban and white. All three are in the same industrial metropolitan area, yet were studied at different times. Cusick argues, however, that each of these schools shares a structure common to public high schools in the United States: the same patterns, problems, and solutions. He claims that they also share the same theme: "the egalitarian ideal." Finally, all three schools share a local context that Cusick contends involves "growth, industrialization, and movement." As industry grew, new immigrants moved into the area and eventually improved their social class standing. The ethnic divisions at the time of Cusick's study involved race. The schools were implicated in this division initially through segregation and then through desegregation. Cusick argues that "biracialism" in the three high schools was an emotional issue. It led to a number of racial incidents that threatened to "escalate" and damage the "maintenance of public confidence." Nonetheless, the administration attempted to address biracialism indirectly because biracialism and racial animosity prevented a "consensual basis" for schooling. "Bound by the egalitarian ideal," the administration's approach was to "keep the lid on" through treating biracialism as an issue of "attendance and discipline." Given limited discipline options, maintaining good "personal relations" with students was the vehicle through which the administration attempted to get students in school. Through an "open elective system," they attempted to make the "positive knowledge . . . appealing."

Since positive knowledge itself was not appealing to students, the curriculum reflected the attempt to "get along with the kids" by offering a range of electives to "find something of interest to students." In these classes, teachers relied on "personal relations" to establish "mutual liking" for the purpose of maintaining order and allowing some instruction to take place. The teachers were "free" to create the curriculum and their instruction in response to what "students need." They justified their curricular choices as "good for kids." The teachers competed for resources and students through an "entrepreneurial approach" rather than through cooperation. Having "complex lives" of "outside interests," often involving second jobs, enabled teachers to respond to "mundane" school activities.

Cusick argues that "the dominating element of the schools . . . was their obligation to the egalitarian ideal." This ideal, composed of unappealing positive knowledge, he claims, led to "getting along with kids" as a dominant vehicle and justification in public high schools.

It is apparent that each of these ethnographies can be translated into one another only with some difficulty. Everhart sees the school's role to be one of proletarianization through a structure of reified knowledge and routinization. This is turn engenders the regenerative knowledge of students as they create a culture to fill the void caused by waiting for instruction. The student's culture, as a release for estrangement, serves a reproductive function because it does not challenge the structure, but only fills structural voids. On the other hand, Cusick sees the school's role as assimilation, and the structure of the school as involving an "egalitarian ideal" in the face of "biracialism" and its threat to the "public's confidence" in education. This, in turn, leads to a focus on order, electives, personal relations, and teacher isolation. It is evident that Everhart's and Cusick's explanations are of differing things. Everhart explains student culture; Cusick explains the staff culture. These studies are not simply additive.

METAPHORS FOR REFUTATIONAL SYNTHESIS

Cusick's (1985a) review of Everhart's study is essentially a "naturally inherent" critique (see Figure 4.2). That is, Cusick argues that resistance to capitalism is "a heavy analysis to lay on the behavior of junior high school students." While Cusick sees Everhart's account to be a "success," he discounts Everhart's students' reappropriation of control as "antisocial behavior." Cusick also critiques the focus on students. He argues that Everhart "dismissed accounts of administrators' and teachers' behavior" and treats them as "mere unwitting tools of capitalist oppression." The result is "stereotypic" and does not take into account the resistance of teachers. Cusick concludes by saying we should not dismiss Everhart's analysis, but that Everhart allows his "political statement" to "overwhelm" "alternative inferences."

Everhart's (1985a) review of Cusick's study also has "little quarrel" with the descriptive account. But Everhart critiques Cusick for the

	Everhart concerning Cusick	Cusick concerning Everhart
	(1985a)	(1985a)
Descriptive Analysis:	"little quarrel" (p. 74) "only illustrative" (p. 74)	"success" (p. 70)
Interpretation:	"overly rigid" (p. 74) "adherence to a functionalist approach" (p. 74) "insufficient" (p. 75) supports "natural selection" (p. 75) accepts "the way things are" (p. 75)	"heavy analysis" (p. 70) "overdone" (p. 70) "political statement" (p. 72)
	(1985b)	(1985b)
Role of Theory for Other:	"masks" (p. 248) "underwhelms" (p. 248)	"obscured" (p. 247) "absolved his subjects from responsibility" (p. 247)
Role of Theory for Self:	"explicit(ness)" (p. 248)	enables "description" (p. 247)

Figure 4.2: Metaphors for Refutational Synthesis

"illustrative," rather than in-depth, use of central actors and (like Cusick's critique) for an "overdone" interpretation. His most severe critique is reserved for the "overly rigid adherence to a functionalist approach" that Everhart argues "seems insufficient." Further, he claims that Cusick describes an "egalitarian ideology" rather than an ideal that seems to support a "'natural' selection process." Everhart also sees the funtionalist model as limited. He contends that the legitimation process is a "dynamic" in which both staff and students are "victims" and accept "the way things are" as "inevitable."

Cusick (1985b) comments on the exchange. While admitting the "weakness of functional analysis," he argues functionalism is more "pertinent" than Everhart's approach. Further, Cusick argues that he is "not obligated to use it," attributing the choice of theoretical model to be a "preference." Functionalism, to Cusick, enabled "descriptions," while Everhart's theory "obscured" them. Further, he believes Everhart's analysis "absolved his subjects from any responsibility." In any case, says Cusick, the point is to describe, not to analyze, as "analysis should be kept as light as possible."

Everhart's (1985b) comment focuses on "differences of opinion" about interpretation. He argues that Cusick's political statements "underwhelm" his interpretations. The central disagreement, Everhart argues, is how "explicit" premises are and what their role should be in interpretation. To Everhart, Cusick "masks" his political statement.

The refutations contained in this exchange can be translated more easily into one another than the account themselves. Cusick's refutation of Everhart is based in Cusick's presumption that the purpose of theory is to facilitate "descriptions." On the other hand, Everhart's refutation of Cusick is based in his presumption that theory is a political statement. Each chides the other for accepting his subjects on his own terms, albeit different subjects and different terms. Yet each "recognizes" the descriptive account of the other as reasonable.

Our approach in this chapter enables us to complete the meta-ethnographic synthesis by combining the two metaphoric reductions (see Figure 4.3). We can argue that each researcher's theory is ideology to the other and that each theory/ideology explains the description. Each is a "reading" of culture (Geertz, 1973). For Cusick, the formal structure is legitimate, but struggles with constraints. For Everhart, the formal structure is struggling for legitimacy. For Cusick, the schools and classrooms are the "natural" result of pursuing the egalitarian ideal. For Everhart, schools and classrooms impede egalitarianism by their purpose and structure. For Cusick, the staff are doing the best they can under the existing conditions and, for Everhart, the students are doing likewise. Yet Cusick's schools and classrooms are not those of Everhart. Each sees a different thing when he conducts research.

As is apparent, the metaphors of neither Cusick nor Everhart are sufficient to account for those of the other. A new set of metaphors is necessary for us to synthesize the refutations and the ethnographies. While this was also true in the "Crisis of Authority" synthesis in Chapter 3, here the synthesis reveals much more about the theoretical foundations of ethnography and its intimate relationship with interpretation.

The value of refutational synthesis, then, is that it allows us to determine directly how ideas affect interpretations. This lesson is reinforced by the Derek Freeman-Margaret Mead synthesis that follows.

The Freeman Refutation of Mead

Anthropological controversies rarely reach the media. One exception is Derek Freeman's (1983) refutation of Margaret Mead's *Coming of Age in Samoa* (1928). A popular anthropologist, Margaret Mead, and a

	Everhart	Cusick
Context:	theory as explicit political statement	theory as description
Formal Structure:	struggle for legitimacy	legitimacy struggling with constraints
Classroom Dynamics:	impede egalitarianism through social reproduction	natural result of pursuing egalitarian ideal
Substructure:	making the best of it	making the best of it

Figure 4.3: Combined Synthesis

popular perspective, that of cultural determinism, were being challenged. While Margaret Mead was not alive to respond to Freeman, it is evident that Mead's work was itself a refutation of the eugenics movement and its extreme biological determinism. Further, her basic question refers not only to the culture of Samoa, but also to the culture of the United States. She asked:

Are the disturbances that vex our adolescents due to the nature of adolescence itself or to the civilization? Under different conditions does adolescence present a different picture? [p. 11].

She sought evidence to prove that the "effects of civilization" produce the stressful adolescence seen in the West. Her proof, she believed, rested in the "tale of the groups of girls with whom I spent many months." Since Freeman's work is also explicitly a refutation, it seems appropriate not to separate the refutations from the accounts, at least initially. They are intertwined.

Mead opens her account with a distinction between the activities of the day and those of the night. "Day is the time for the councils of old men and the labours of youth," and night is the time for "lighter things." The early education of Samoan children, especially for the young girls, is that of learning the "essential avoidances" and preparing for the responsibility of "baby-tending." Boys are involved in baby-tending only for a short time and then move into male peer groups to learn "effective cooperation." The girls have a "high standard of individual responsibility," but "no lessons in cooperation." Adolescent girls, as soon as they are able "to carry heavy loads," are "released from baby-

	Mead (1928)	Freeman (1984)
Refutation:	"effects of civilization" (p. 6)	"testing" (Mead's account) (p. xii) "scientific adequacy" (p. 83)
Perspective:	"tale of a group of girls" (p. 131) American Samoa	cultural determinism as "dogma" (p. 5) "historical" (p. 114) "active member of a Fono" (p. xiv) a later Western Samoa
Childrearing:	"essential avoidances" (p. 26) "diffusion of affections" (p. 210)	"stringent discipline" (p. 205) "attachment" (p. 203)
Childhood for girls:	"baby tending" (p. 26) "so little is mysterious, so little forbidden" (p. 137) "high standard of individual responsibility" (p. 27) "no lessons in cooperation (p. 27) "antagonism" toward boys (p. 59)	
Adolescence for girls:	"released from baby-tending" (p. 28) "complicated techniques" (p. 29) of: "preparing food" (p. 29) "fishing" (p. 30) "weaving" (p. 31) "I am but young" (p. 33) "clandestine sex adventures" (p. 33) "maids of honor" (p. 76) "general social negligence" (p. 82) "insouciance" about "social organization" (p. 82) deviance as: "more choice than is traditionally possible" (p. 171) "deviation from group standards" (p. 183)	
Maturity for women:	"increase her value as a wife" (p. 185) "performing skilled tasks" (p. 193)	
Childhood for boys:	"baby-tending" (p. 20) "effective cooperation" (p. 27) "strict avoidance" (p. 44) of girls	

Figure 4.4: Freeman-Mead Refutational Synthesis

Adolescence for boys:	"badgered into efficiency by rivalry, precept and example" (p. 34)	"tension" (p. 219)
	"spurred to greater efforts" (p. 37)	"psychological disturbances" (p. 225)
	"institutionalized relationships" (p.69)	"offenses against authority" (p. 260)
Maturity for men:	"years of striving" (p. 190)	"aggressive" (p. 172)
	"title" (p. 191)	"warlike" (p. 172)
	"disqualified" (p. 193)	"absolute obedience" (p. 192)
		"severe punishment in interests of obedience and respect for authority" (p. 198)
		"insistent demands of their society" (p. 274)
		"personal courage" (p. 269)
Sexual Relations:	"free and easy experimentation" (p. 98)	"cult of virginity" (p. 239)
	"a very brittle monogamy" (p. 108)	
Dance:	"offsets the rigorous subordination of children" (p. 117)	
	"reduction in threshold of shyness" (p. 118)	
Rank:	"never ending source of interest" (p. 50)	"aggressively safeguarded and meticulously observed" (p. 140)
	"indirectly" affects children (p. 50)	"competitive" (p. 156)
		"direct oracular communication" with the gods (p. 176)
Explanation:	"lack of deep feeling" (p. 199)	"deep-seated ambivalence" (p. 211) toward authority
	"lack of personal relationship" (p. 215)	"respect and love alternating with resentment and fear" (p. 276)
	"sex feeling" (p. 215)	
	"place of work and play in children's lives" (p. 226)	
	"lack of pressure to make choices"	
Implications:	"training our children for the choices" (p. 246)	"more scientific anthropological paradigm" (p. 294)
	"how to think, not what to think" (p. 246)	"genetic and exogentic" (p. 299)
	"tolerance" (p. 246)	

Figure 4.4 Continued

tending." They then begin to learn "the more complicated techniques" such as "preparing food," "fishing," and "weaving." An adolescent girl may avoid serious responsibilities with the justification, "I am but young." At the same time, "all of her interest is expended on clandestine sex adventures."

The adolescent boy is subject to the "Aumaga," the male peer group, and the process of earning rank and title. He is "badgered into efficiency by rivalry, precept, and example." The boy is "spurred to greater efforts."

Samoan households are presided over by a "matai," a head man, where "age rather than relationship gives disciplinary authority." This "enormous diffusion of authority" is coupled with the children "testing out other possible residences." Relatives have a "most rigid code of etiquette prescribed" for their social relations, starting with "strict avoidance" of the opposite sex among the young. For the adults of the household, "rank" is "a never-failing source of interest." Yet, for the children, rank only "indirectly" affects their lives.

As children grow older, "voluntary association" in sex-specific groups is evident. "Antagonism" between the young boys and girls is evident. The "gangs" are based, for both boys and girls, in "the double bonds of neighborhood and relationship." For older girls, "relationship" and "similar sex interests" are the basis of friendships. But by the time of puberty for these girls, the "individual nature of tasks" and the "need for secrecy in their amatory adventures" end voluntary forms of association. For older boys, "institutionalized relationships" exist to establish cooperation that "lasts through life."

The community "ignores" the girls and boys until sometime after puberty, when they are grouped into organizations, "Aumaga" for the young men, "Aualuma" for the young women, and wives of untitled men and widows. The "Aumaga," the "Aualuma" and women without titled husbands are all "echoes of the central political structure of the village, the *Fono*." The "Aumaga" "mirrors" the organization of older men, while the "Aualuma" forms "a group of maids of honor" for the village princess. "Taking their status from their husbands," women and girls repay "the general social negligence" they receive with "insouciance" about the "intricacies of the social organization."

Dance in American Samoa "offsets the rigorous subordination of children" and results in a "reduction of the threshold of shyness."

Mead writes that there are three types of sexual relations recognized by the community: "formal marriage," "love affairs between unmarried young people" and "adultery." Moreover, there are three forms of relationships among the unmarried: "the clandestine encounter," "the published elopement," and "sleep crawling." For most youth, sex is "free and easy experimentation" and marriage "a very brittle monogamy."

For Mead, coming of age in Samoa, "where so little is mysterious, so little forbidden," represented "no period of crisis or stress, but was instead an orderly developing of a set of slowly maturing interests and activities." For the girl, this lack of conflict was the result of an "absence of any important institutionalized relationships." There were exceptions to this, however. A few girls "deviated" by "exercis[ing] more choice than is traditionally permissible" or "deviat[ing] from group standards."

In maturity, a woman seeks "to increase her value as a wife" through childbearing and a titled husband. For young men, adulthood signifies "years of striving" for entrance into the *Fono*. Old age for women involves "performing skilled tasks," while for old men, being "disqualified" from the *Fono* looms. In the end, old women are "more of a power with the household than the old men."

Mead follows her account by returning to her original question and concludes that, unlike American adolescence, Samoan adolescence is not stressful. This is due to a "lack of deep feeling," a "lack of personal relationships," "diffusion of affection," the "sex feeling," the "place of work and play in the children's lives," and the "lack of pressure to make choices." In contrast, Mead depicts American culture as having "different and mutually exclusive standards" and "a world of choices." It is as if "each family group is fighting a battle" of its standards versus those of others. As a result, Mead argues that education in the United States should train children "for the choices that will confront them": "how to think, not what to think," and "tolerance."

Derek Freeman (1983) is not as concerned with constructing an ethnographic account as he is concerned with "testing" the "scientific adequacy" of Mead's ethnography. Freeman's testing begins some 17 years later than Mead's and is based on "Western Samoa." Additionally, the account is "historical," being based in official archives and accounts of missionaries and others, as well as in Freeman's direct research as an "adopted son" and "active member of the Sa'anapu *Fono*." Freeman portrays Mead's study as an attempt to provide the "absolute truth of cultural determinism" to Franz Boaz. Boaz and others, according to Freeman, had so dissociated cultural anthropology from biology as to raise cultural determinism to a "dogma." Freeman portrays Mead's research as a "homespun approach," with limited access to "informants." These factors, he claims, allowed her to "overlook evidence counter to her beliefs."

Freeman's testing of Mead's account is a series of refutations of selected interpretations of Mead. He argues that Mead has "numerous misconceptions" about *Fono* behavior and the "sanctity" of the rank system. Freeman claims that for Samoan men, rank is "aggressively safeguarded and meticulously observed." Freeman finds Samoan men to be "highly competitive" concerning issues of rank and ceremony. He describes them as "aggressive" and "warlike," "highly religious" in their "direct oracular communication" with their gods, and expressive of "guilt" in affairs of rank and ceremony. For men, "absolute obedience" to "chiefly instruction" was enforced by "severe punishment in the interests of obedience and respect for authority."

Freeman counters Mead's depiction of child rearing with a portrait of strong "attachment" of child to mother and "stringent discipline." This, he argues, creates a "deep seated ambivalence" toward authority, "respect and love alternating with resentment and fear." He sees Samoans as "an intensely emotional people" with a "controlled aloofness" that hides their feelings. Such "tension" results in "psychological disturbances." Freeman finds Samoa a "cult of virginity" around the ceremonial virgins.

Adolescents in Samoa, for Freeman, are subjected to "psychological stress" evidenced by "offenses against authority." Freeman finds Samoan males very concerned with "personal courage," unable to escape the "insistent demands of their society" and "the custom of inflicting punishment to maintain social order."

Freeman sums up his refutation, noting that Mead's "misconstruing of Samoa" is due to her "avowed cultural determinism." This, he argues, can be best remedied by a "more scientific anthropological paradigm" having a view of human evolution that incorporates both "the genetic and exogenetic."

In closely examining Figure 4.4, we can see that it is difficult to translate these studies into one another. This is for rather different reasons than we found with the Cusick and Everhart synthesis. As described, the Cusick and Everhart refutations indicate that theory is used quite differently. For Mead and Freeman, the difficulty rests in the fact that each study is from a particular perspective. Mead gives a "tale of a group of girls," while Freeman's "reading" of culture is based on his study of official documents and the political lives of men. Surprisingly, given Freeman's intent, the studies are not fully parallel. Freeman establishes not that Mead misconstrued Samoa, but that the world views of women and men are quite different. Women have no adolescent crisis because of social negligence. Men have institutionalized relationships of rivalry and obedience in the affairs of rank and politics and, therefore, experience psychological disturbances.

Even when they disagree, it is possible to translate one understanding into the other. Mead's portrayal of male adolescence effectively describes the basis for the symptoms of "tension" that Freeman finds. Freeman's portrayal of maturity in males reveals the dynamics of the "striving" Mead saw. The explanations each offers for Samoan culture can also be translated into one another. Free experimentation in practice and a cult of virginity for ceremonial purposes are not necessarily at odds. The "lack of deep feeling" that Mead observed may well be the same as Freeman's "ambivalence."

The refutations that Mead and Freeman each propose are not easily translatable. Mead's "negative instance" demonstrates that culture has an effect, even if it does not provide the "absolute answer," as she hoped. Freeman, on the other hand, neither directly refutes Mead's evidence nor demonstrates that "nature" has effects. Intriguingly, our synthesis reveals Freeman's refutation to be as dogmatic as he critiqued Mead's to be. To return to Mead's opening metaphor, Freeman's study is a study of day, the councils of men and the labours of youth; Mead's study is of the night, of lighter things (albeit a poor metaphor for today's audience).

The refutational synthesis in this case reveals that our original assumption about interpretations that refute one another is questionable. First, these two account have points of overlap, but are about substantially different aspects of Samoan life. The metaphors each provides for their respective aspects of Samoan life seem fully adequate. Second, at points of overlap, the interpretations of Mead and of Freeman are complementary in that one describes Samoan culture from the perspectives of women and the other from the perspectives of men. Witness our use of Mead's metaphor for the synthesis. Despite the larger claims of each author, the studies are not refutational. That neither Mead nor Freeman accomplished a full refutation of the paradigm they attacked raises some interesting questions. These questions challenge ethnographers to be aware of their belief systems and how these affect their ability to discern the meaning of their interpretations. Obviously, refutational syntheses enable us to get to the very heart of social thought and research.

Conclusion

Synthesizing refutations is an involved procedure that teaches us much about the assumptions that guide various studies. In examining the accounts and debate of Cusick and Everhart, we learn that they are constructing interpretations under very different rules. We also see that the variances in their accounts are due to these rules. From Freeman and Mead, we learn that refutation may be based in the study of rather different aspects of a culture, despite an author's wish to generalize to the culture as a whole. From both cases, we discover that refutations may be driven by dogma and that refutations of such dogma may be dogmatic in themselves. Finally, taken together, the accounts and refutations undermine each author's claim that one perspective is sufficient to explain an ethnographic account. If the descriptions are reasonable, but the interpretations are ideological, then we must focus on multiple interpretations (Douglas, 1976) as a solution.

5. LINES-OF-ARGUMENT SYNTHESIS

In Chapter 3, we developed the thesis that a meta-ethnographic approach can be understood as the reciprocal translation of studies. We addressed syntheses of studies that seemingly refute each other in Chapter 4. There is a type of interpretive synthesis, however, that is more concerned with inference and is amenable to the meta-ethnographic approach. This is a lines-of-argument synthesis. A lines-of-argument synthesis is essentially about inference: What can we say of the whole (organization, culture, etc.), based on selective studies of the parts? This is the same as basic theorizing in qualitative research and is conceptualized alternatively as clinical inference and grounded theorizing.

Clinical Inference

In anthropology, Clifford Geertz (1973: 27) argues that "the office of theory is to provide a vocabulary in which what symbolic action has to say about itself . . . can be expressed." He asserts that it makes no sense to write a general interpretive theory, as theory in ethnography is intended to make thick description possible: "Analysis, then, is the sorting out of the structures of signification . . . and determining their social ground and import" (p. 9).

To accomplish this, Geertz points to a parallel with "clinical inference (p. 26) in medicine and depth psychology. As he explains, "such inference begins with a set of (presumptive) signifiers and attempts to place them within an intelligible frame" (p. 26). While he notes that the purpose of such theorizing is different in therapy than in social science, they are the same in the sense that theory is used in each "to ferret out the unapparent import of things" (p. 26).

A lines-of-argument synthesis, following Geertz's formulation, draws from studies the "structures of signification" both within each study *and* for studies as a set. Like clinical inference, the goal of lines-of-argument synthesis is to discover a "whole" among a set of parts. Like ethnographic accounts, it is emic (Spicer, 1976) in its allegiance to the studies being synthesized; it is historical in that it uses time to give order and history-in-use to give context; it is comparative in that it constructs an analogy of the relationships among studies; and it is holistic in that it constructs an interpretation of all the studies, their interrelations, and contexts.

Grounded Theorizing

In sociology, Glaser and Strauss (1967) propose a "general method of comparative analysis" (p. 1). For them, adequate theory must both "fit" and "work."

> By "fit" we mean that the categories must be readily (not forcibly) applicable to and indicated by the data under study; by "work" we mean that they must be meaningfully relevant to and be able to explain the behavior under study [p. 3].

Theories that fit and work are the result, according to Glaser and Strauss, of a "constant comparative method:"

> The constant comparing of many groups draws the sociologist's attention to their similarities and differences. Considering these leads him to generate abstract categories and their properties [p. 36].

The "integrating scheme" (p. 41) that results must encompass all the data and also be "open-ended" enough to allow consideration of new data and conceptual levels. This integrating scheme is delineated through the constant comparisons. First, grounded theory solidifies by requiring fewer and fewer modifications to encompass new data and new comparisons. Second, the researcher may find "underlying uniformities" (p. 110) that enable the theory to be reformulated, allowing for both greater "parsimony" and greater "scope" (p. 111). Third, the scheme becomes "theoretically saturated" (p. 111) in that new incidents and comparisons reveal no new categories or relations.

A lines-of-argument synthesis, following Glaser and Strauss, is accomplished by repeated comparisons between studies. Through discovering the similarities and differences among the studies to be synthesized, an integrating scheme is constructed. This integrating scheme is the synthesis of these dissimilar but related studies. Glaser and Strauss also suggest criteria for adequate lines-of-argument synthesis: They should "fit," "work," be parsimonious, have sufficient scope, and be "theoretically saturated."

Lines of Argument and Meta-Ethnography

Clinical inference and grounded theorizing are each bases for a lines-of-argument synthesis. Both rely on the examination of similarities and differences between cases and on holistic schemes to integrate these. Using our meta-ethnographic approach, we can translate these studies into one another. A lines-of-argument synthesis goes one step further and puts any similarities and dissimilarities into a new interpretive context. In short, the translation of cases into one another sets the stage for a second-level inference about the relationship between the studies. It is the second-level inference that assigns interpretive significance to each study to be synthesized.

A lines-of-argument synthesis involves two steps: a meta-ethnographic synthesis of the studies and a clinical inference about the "whole" line of argument. We first translate the studies into one another. Then we develop a grounded theory that puts the similarities and differences between studies into an interpretive order. In what follows, we return to the desegregation ethnographies to give an example of a lines-of-argument synthesis.

The Desegregation Ethnographies Synthesis

As you will recall from Chapter 1, the failure to achieve an adequate synthesis in the desegregation ethnographies was the impetus for this book. The two synthesis attempts employed an aggregative theory of social explanation and, consequently, stripped context from the case. A meta-ethnography proceeds from rather different assumptions about how to synthesize ethnographies, and enables a new synthesis where other attempts fail.

The desegregation ethnographies synthesis could reasonably be a reciprocal translation, rather than a line-of-argument synthesis. Each of the five accounts could be translated into the others. From that, we would learn a lot about schools and communities, school cultures, classroom processes, race relations, and so on. Yet the desegregation ethnographies were all undertaken to "say something" about school desegregation, to infer from particular studies something about school desegregation as a social phenomenon. Each study may be seen as an artifact of the school desegregation debate in our original study. Taken together, the desegregation ethnographies should enable a line of argument about the nature of school desegregation in the United States.

To construct our line of argument, we will use Ray Rist's (1979) collection of the five studies discussed earlier. This collection is ideal for our purpose since the intent of the volume, as indicated by the title, is to give multiple "appraisals of an American experiment" with school desegregation. It was in this volume that the ethnographers intended to "say something" about school desegregation, in that "each school is like all other schools, like some other schools, and like no other schools" (Rist, 1979: 7).

The volume arranges the studies in two sets of three chapters each: "The Southern Experience" and "The Northern Experience." The Southern Experience has two of its three chapters drawn from one study, albeit focused on rather different issues. The other chapters are from separate studies. The key metaphors for the studies are displayed in Figures 5.1a and 5.1b.

For two years, Clement et al. (1979) studied the "social race relations" found in an elementary school, Grandin School. The school was in a southern city (p. 17) characterized as having "separate systems" of blacks and whites. "Fearing violence and civil disorders," local political struggles were kept "backstage" but revealed the "increasing power of the black community." In this context, school district policies reflected "avoidance of conflict" via (1) a "delay in institutional differentiation" until after the elementary school years, and (2) "explicit procedures" limiting the use of race as a criteria in official action.

Grandin School had a "complex and tenuous organization of social race relations." Formally, "the category of social race is used only as permitted by the district." Informally, race was an "important category." On this informal level, there were "separating words" to distinguish race. These were not discussed because of the "deemphasis on explicit invocation of social-race identities" that was part of a "norm against provoking conflicts." When "symbolic encounters" about race occurred

	Clement, Eisenhart and Harding (1979)	Noblit (1979)	Collins (1979)
INTENT	"Social race" (p. 16)	"vehicles of public policy ... to amend the political economy" (p. 65) "massive task" (p. 67) of principal	"student subsystem" (p. 102) "boundary maintenance" (p. 90)
SETTING	Southern City elementary school (p. 17) "separate systems" (p. 18) "fearing violence" (p. 19) "increasing power of black community" (p. 19)	Southern City high school (p. 68)	Southern City high school (p. 89) whites "negative" (p. 89) and "withdrew" (p. 89) "racial and labor strife" (p. 93) "extreme animosity" (p. 92)
SCHOOL DISTRICT	"avoidance of conflict" (p. 20)	"keep the lid on" (p. 68)	"attempting to recover" (p. 89) "strong vested interests" (p. 93)
SCHOOL	"complex and tenuous ... social race relations" (p. 23) formal: race "only as permitted" (p. 23) informal: "separating words" (p. 24) "norm against provoking conflicts" (p. 33) "tension," "repeated needless errors" (p. 42)	"Patience" (p. 67) "fishbowl" (p. 68) "marked man" (p. 68) "declared war" (p. 71) "Prudence" (p. 67) "pragmatic" (p. 73) "uneasy, quiet, and closed" (p. 74)	"early edge" (p. 102) of whites "school flight" (p. 102) "evolve in favor of black students" (p. 102) "ethnic control" (p. 106)

CONSEQUENCES	"norms" (p. 49):
	  "apply to overt behavior" (p. 49)
	  "teacher responsibility" (p. 50)
	  "polite conversation" (p. 50)
	  "informal segregation"
	
	harmony "only so deep" (p. 61)
		"Patience": "negotiated order" (p. 76) "peace bond" (p. 79) "two schools" (p. 79)
		
		"Prudence": "bureaucratic order" (p. 80) "his roles" (p. 82) "low profile" (p. 84) "black" school (p. 81)
			"Control" is "rigid maintenance of boundaries" (p. 113)

LINE OF ARGUMENT	"could be much worse" (p. 61) "blacks have begun to achieve representation" (p. 61)	not "two tales of failure" (p. 85) "may not be possible to make it acceptable to whites" (p. 86)	"did not erode racial boundaries" (p. 112)

Figure 5.1a: School Desegregation Synthesis, "The Southern Experience"

	Scherer and Slawski (1979)	Schofield and Sagar (1979)	Sullivan (1979b)
INTENT	"avoid pitfalls" (p. 117)	"social learning" (p. 155)	"to define" (p. 201) desegregation
	"strategies of control" (p. 118)		"cultural contact" (p. 202)
	"unanticipated consequences" (p. 118)		
SETTING	Northern City high school (p. 117)	Northern City middle school (p. 157)	New York City high school (p. 202)
	"lowest point" (p. 119)	"variety of ethnic groups" (p. 157)	"waves of immigrants" (p. 202)
	"bitter busing controversy" (p. 119)	"heavily segregated" (p. 157)	"school wars" (p. 203)
	"emerging political power of black leadership" (p. 120)		
SCHOOL DISTRICT	desegregation "improved overall quality" (p. 121)	"without considerable busing" (p. 158)	"school people as an interest group" (p. 203)
	"protect gains" (p. 121)		"absorption" (p. 203) or "ethnic succession" (p. 203)
SCHOOL	"prison-like" (p. 122)	"a model of high quality integrated education" (p. 158)	"two neighborhoods" (p. 204)
	"unlimited hiding places" (p. 123)	"equal formal status" (p. 158)	"controlled by central office" (p. 206)
	"earlier period of violence" (p. 123)	"segregation" (p. 158)	"stereotypical categorization" (p. 207)
		"avoid fostering competition" (p. 160)	"programming" as "control" (p. 207)
		"academics first" (p. 161)	"ethnic boundaries" (p. 209)
		"natural progression assumption" (p. 164)	"handicapped" (p. 209)
		"colorblind" (p. 166)	
CONSEQUENCE	"teacher isolation" (p. 124)	equal status contact: "very close" (p. 170)	"personal networks" (p.217): "neighborhood" (p. 218)
	"avoidance of violence" (p. 140)	Cooperation: "unlikely" (p. 176)	"ethnicity" (p. 219)
	"avoid challenges" (p. 147)	"acquaintance potentials" (p. 176) "likely to cause problems" (p. 176)	"social class" (p. 219) "status within school" (p. 220)
	"fewer biracial contacts" (p. 148)		"structural assimiliation" (p. 223)
	"concerns at school" (p. 148)		
	"one-to-one" (p. 148)		
LINE OF ARGUMENT	"instance of larger societal struggles" (p. 118)	"not sufficient to ensue positive social learning" (p. 196)	"image of the future" (p. 201)
	"given over to rhetoric" (p. 153)		desegregation as "manipulation of political power" (p. 236)

Figure 5.1b: School Desegregation Synthesis, "The Northern Experience"

(with "relative infrequency"), they were "generally negative," with high "ambiguity." The ambiguity was due to the existence of "multiple interpretations" of the encounter and "cultural differences" in what was demeaning. The result of this was "tension" and "repeated needless errors" in cross-race interaction. It also engendered "norms" that "apply to overt behavior," "the primacy of teacher responsibility for the student," and "polite cooperation." These norms allowed "informal segregation."

Clement et al. (1979) use the metaphor of "harmony" to discuss cross-race relations. "In support of harmony" are norms about "polite cooperation," "rule pluralism," "emphasis on social class" in explanations, and "withdrawal." Yet, harmony was "only so deep" because it was "achieved by social mechanisms rather than by personal ties."

For Clement et al. (1979) it "could be much worse." There are "few positive models" for desegregation, and at Grandin "obvious patterns of discrimination are absent." Moreover, "blacks have begun to achieve representation" at all levels of the school system.

Noblit (1979) argued that desegregation was "an issue of the political economy" in which schools were "destined to be the vehicles of public policy . . . to amend the political economy." Indeed, local debate focused more on "political and economic implications than upon educational issues." This meant that the principal of a desegregated school had the "massive task" to "manage a complex set of pressures and forces" in the face of "success [that] has various meanings." Following Wolcott (1973), Noblit argued that there are two orientations to the principalship: "patience" ("a concern with the normative, ethical, and moral") and "prudence" ("a concern with the practical and functional"). As a "man in the middle," "his freedom was to make no serious mistakes" (Wolcott, 1973: 306).

In the southern urban high school of Noblit's case, a change in principals, with dramatically different styles, enabled a comparison of what "patience" and "prudence" meant in a desegregated high school. "Patience" was the first principal. Under his leadership, the school was a "fishbowl on how desegregation can work" and, as a result, "Patience" viewed himself as a "marked man." Since desegregation meant both "keep(ing) the lid on" and "retaining . . . white students," Patience allowed the white "old guard" teachers and "honor students" "considerable influence" in the affairs of the school. This influence was threatened by declining white enrollments, inciting an incident in which the honor students "declared war" via a "mobilization of their elite parents." The "search" for the "basic issue" and a "direct white line" to the school board led to a decision that what was needed was a "principal who would enforce the bureaucracy." "Prudence" fit this bill. He was "pragmatic" and a "tough cookie." He ran a "tight ship," being "very visible and very coercive." Under the focus on "discipline," the "school became uneasy, quiet, and closed." White students and teachers increasingly left the school via various "transfers."

Noblit proposed that the "administrative styles" of Patience and Prudence were different "characterizations of order" involving "rules" and "deterrence." The "negotiated order" of Patience sought legitimacy as the "product of a peace bond" via "negotiable" rules and "student's personal indebtedness to the principal." Peace involved "two schools . . . under one roof" (one black and one white) and the freedom to "express opinions quite freely." The peace was broken, and a war declared. The "bureaucratic order" of Prudence assumed rules to be "legitimate," and a deterrent. Under "his rules," the teachers sought a "low profile" and the school became "black" in identity.

For Noblit, these are not "two tales of failure," for each principal was "indeed successful": Each did achieve what he sought. In conclusion, he argues that "in as much as desegregation challenges white supremacy, it may not be possible to make it acceptable to whites."

Collins (1979) was coprincipal investigator with Noblit but focused his chapter primarily on the context and the students. His purpose was to report the extent to which desegregation had "affected social relationships." Collins argued that the reaction to desegregation among whites was "expectably negative" and, therefore, they "withdrew" from the school system. The district was "attempting to recover" by efforts to "stabilize social relationships." In Memphis, where "opportunities for interclass mobility are limited," "a long agonizing decade" of "severe racial and labor strife" meant "extreme animosity now reigns where once some racial tolerance existed." This led to an "insular" and "defensive" school district with "strong vested interests that distort the real education issues." The courts and the black community concluded that the district was "not demonstrating good faith" in desegregation. "Black frustration" and the assassination of Martin Luther King led to "a spread-the-misery campaign" of "black Monday boycotts." The "continuing confrontation" gave students "grave expectations of their future in education."

As indicated by Noblit (1979), desegregation meant the "pairing" of two schools, each of which was a "unifying force" in their respective communities. The historically white, "college prep school" became the desegregated high school. As Collins (1979) argued, the white students had an "early edge": "They knew the territory." It was perceived that the "strong competitive system" had "slipped." The "status deprivation" of the whites who remained promoted ongoing "school flight."

In this context, Collins focused on the "student subsystem" and "boundary maintenance" within it. While control continued to "evolve in the favor of the black students," student activities were largely arenas of "ethnic control." Only in band and ROTC was there "racial mixing." In ROTC, such mixing "carried the greatest potential for violence." In general, however, "control" of the student system was "the rigid maintenance of boundaries separating blacks and whites." In conclusion, Collins argued that desegregation "did not erode the racial boundaries in the student subsystem."

Scherer and Slawski (1979) studied one of the first northern cities ordered to use "busing" so that others might "avoid pitfalls." Their study focused on the "strategies of control that characterized Pawnee West," a high school. The "assumption of this control strategy" was that the desegregation was "an episodic event" that produced "unanticipated consequences" in the school. "Control" ("efforts to control events and their interpretation") was the "dominant theme," but was carried out with "varied tactics" in the school. This, Scherer and Slawski argue, was "one instance of larger societal struggles and debates over power, opportunity, and freedom."

Pawnee was a "poor" city, a "small town in outlook and rhythm" in which industrial growth had been "restricted with poor prognosis." At the "lowest point in Pawnee's development," desegregation occurred as a "bitter busing controversy" amid the "emerging political power of black leadership." Desegregation was best seen "both as a result of the changes and at the same time a stimulant for even more change."

Pawnee West High School was a new building "closely interwoven" with desegregation. Its location was a "compromise" between blacks and whites. It was believed that desegregation had "improved the overall quality of education." Yet to the community, the "fragile quality of desegregation and the necessity to protect the gains accomplished" were both apparent. Pawnee West was a "prison-like" building amid an "attractive and spacious campus" where few students could "experience a sense of privacy" but were afforded "unlimited" hiding places. The school was also imbued with a "memory of an earlier period of violence" that "gives particular meaning to the issue of control."

"Several unintended, and apparently unanticipated, consequences occurred." These included: "teacher isolation," "a reputation that includes violence," efforts to "limit . . . the opportunities for confrontation" by eliminating lunch and many extra-curricular activities, and a "decline in academic standards." Nonetheless, the school remained an "athletic powerhouse."

At Pawnee West, the "currency of control" was "space and time." "Official time" was "rigidly scheduled" and "student time . . . organized around the constraints of official time." For those "who seek more freedom," the school offered "many avenues of escape." Students could "negotiate" to "accumulate more student time" and practiced "avoidance" via various forms of "skipping." Students were also socialized to the "avoidance of violence." Especially for whites being "hassled" by blacks, "the understood rules" were "mind your own business and avoid risks." The "consequences of avoidance" were that students "avoid challenges" and have "fewer biracial contacts." Students largely coped with desegregation by "dealing with other concerns at school" and "one-to-one" friendships.

Pawnee West had "another strategy for controlling uncertainty"— "rhetoric." This rhetoric was threefold: (1) desegregation was treated as "an accomplished fact," (2) a "people get along here" rhetoric obscured "the persistence of racial concerns," and (3) interracial schooling was portrayed as a "taste of real life." Scherer and Slawski argue that debate over desegregation has "obscured the more complex issue of poverty, unemployment, and economic discrimination" and, unless this is addressed, desegregation "is given over to rhetoric," as in Pawnee West.

Schofield and Sagar (1979) focused on "social learning": "The social experiences of children in interracial schools and the impact of these experiences on intergroup attitudes and behavior." The setting was a northern "industrial" city with a "rich variety of ethnic groups" that were "heavily segregated." The school board focused on creating a new school, Wexler Middle School, to "serve as a model of high quality integrated education." To this end, there was "open enrollment" to obtain a "racially balanced" student body.

Schofield and Sagar characterized Wexler via three "criteria for integration." First, the "equal status contact" criteria revealed "equal formal status" with "segregation" in the highest achievement and lowest achievement classes. Second, "cooperation towards shared goals" was evidenced in Wexler's efforts to "avoid fostering competition." Finally, "support for positive relations" was seen as the faculty's consensus that "racially motivated negative behavior should not be tolerated." Nevertheless, it was clear that "academics first" was the "mission" of the school. Indeed, there was an "emphasis on academic work as preventive medicine" for children's personal and social development. This was coupled with (1) "the natural progression assumption" that mere interracial contact promotes positive relations and further that "efforts to promote intergroup interaction will backfire," and (2) "the colorblind perspective" that publicly treats race as "completely irrelevant" while it remains "important" in students' "perceptions" and "behavior." Schofield and Sagar, as a result, characterized the school as being "very close" to achieving equal status contact while the "disparity in academic performance" created a "problem in maintaining" current efforts. With the "academics first" orientation in the school and the students' "strongly individualistic and competitive orientation," however, "cooperation to attain mutually desired goals" was "unlikely." Finally, it seems that even the "acquisition potential" or opportunity for interracial interaction at Wexler was "likely to cause problems."

Schofield and Sagar argued that "classroom practices also influence intergroup learning." "Seating policies," either "voluntary" or "assigned," "tended to result in racially identifiable groups." The authors also identified three "teaching methods" and their effects. They found that (1) the "traditional" method was "inimical to cooperation," (2) the "individualized" method was "conducive to cooperation," and (3) the "group oriented" method "legitimates cooperation," but was the "rarest" to be used.

Schofield and Sagar argued that "the school provides little opportunity for guided learning about group differences" and this "causes intergroup problems." In the end, interracial interaction at Wexler was "not sufficient to ensure positive social learning."

Sullivan (1979b) argued that the debate over school desegregation attests to "its ambiguity and to the fact that, ultimately, the term refers to an image of the future." Furthermore, he claimed that the "greatest service" of qualitative research would be "to define" desegregation. "In the most general sense," desegregation referred to "cultural contact in school systems"; he addressed his study to this issue. Sheridan High School was in New York City. Both the city and the school had been faced with "waves of immigrants" resulting in a history of "school wars" involving a repeated "upsurge in ethnic identification and ideology." This resulted in the "decentralization" of the school district (which had the "unanticipated consequence" of the emergence of "school people as an interest group"). The "process of ethnic succession" was seen as "absorption" by district officials.

Sheridan served primarily "two neighborhoods of the central city." One neighborhood was "polyethnic" and "fragmented," having considerable "population change" because of "immigrants." The other neighborhood was "black," "stable" and "politically well organized." Both the "process in the larger communities" and the "organization of the school" affected the "informal organization of the turfs and networks and social control."

Sheridan was an "academic-comprehensive" high school "controlled by the central office" that in turn was seen as "dominated by members of earlier immigrant groups." At Sheridan, "size" and "ethnic diversity" led to "stereotypical categorization" of students. The "complexity of the curriculum" made "programming" "one of the chief instruments of social control." The principal had both "authority" and a "great deal of discretionary power," and worked to create the "school's image as an orderly place." "Prestigious classes" were ethnically "mixed" and "slow-learners" classes were "entirely minority." "Extra-curricular activities" had "ethnic boundaries." Finally, the faculty was "unionized," "white and Jewish." The school was "handicapped" by "low and erratic" attendance rates leading to "difficulty in maintaining order" and "difficulty in maintaining continuity of instruction."

For students, "personal networks" had "five sources": "neighborhood of residence," "ethnicity," "social class," "status within school," and "activities of special interest." Sullivan argued that "ethnic boundaries are more rigid among lower class members of the ethnic category and among recent immigrants." There were "limited instrumental transactions" across ethnic boundaries. However, "neither class nor ethnicity" was "sufficient to explain differences in school performance." Rather, "structural assimilation" in which students "share with the staff certain assumptions about schooling" was the "most important criterion" for success in school. Such "sorting" of the students involved the "assignment of labels."

In conclusion, Sullivan argued that schools were "powerful interest groups" who acted as "agents of Americanization," even though "new immigrants" were not willing to "surrender their ethnic identity." "Ethnic politics" "dominate(d) both the management of schools and the processes of affiliation among students." This implies that desegregation meant the "manipulation of political power in the community as much as, if not more than, any school-specific changes." Sullivan asked the "ultimate question": Can changes in schools "remedy the problems we identify with segregation and desegregation?"

Conclusion

These elaborations of the metaphors employed in each study reveal that each set is seemingly adequate to summarize its case. Further, the parallels between the cases are many. Treating these cases as reciprocal translations yields a synthesis about the cultural and social organization of urban, desegregated schools. Each school was like the others in that school desegregation took place as part of the political struggle between minorities and whites; in this struggle, the blacks were gaining and the school district was on the defensive. The struggle was so volatile that the fear of violence became paramount to school officials who defined desegregation as equal formal treatment with an emphasis on academics and control. Being "colorblind" (Schofield and Sagar, 1979: 166) meant "repeated needless errors" (Clement et al., 1979: 42) in intergroup relations and informal segregation by achievement grouping. On the other hand, the studies were unlike each other in grade level, region (even the North/South distinction does not hold), degree of ethnicity, and the ways what was significant was revealed.

Each of these studies represents a developing line of argument: some statement about school desegregation as a social phenomena. The line of argument that can be inferred or theorized from these studies is that school desegregation is inappropriately conceived of as an educational issue. While each of the desegregation ethnographies focused on a school, it was apparent that the issues of school were only a microcosm of those in the community. In fact, school desegregation may be better conceived of and assessed by the emergence of minority political leadership in the city and access to education as an employer, interest group, and socializer of youth. In light of these ethnographies, it seems inappropriate to conceive of desegregation as an intervention designed to reduce prejudice or achievement gaps among students. Following this line of argument, school desegregation is successful when "ethnic succession" (Sullivan, 1979b: 203) has taken place, and minorities control the political and educational apparatus of communities, school systems, and schools.

As is evidenced from the synthesis of the desegregation ethnographies, a lines-of-argument synthesis is essentially the construction of an interpretation. It is essentially a process of clinical inference and/or grounded theorizing. While a line of argument is an inference, it also may serve to reveal what is hidden in individual studies. When we compare accounts, metaphors take on new meaning(s), what was hidden becomes apparent; we better understand what was studied by making clinical inferences from the studies.

6. INSCRIBING META-ETHNOGRAPHIES

As noted previously, Geertz (1973: 19) sees interpretivists as "inscribing" a culture when they write their accounts and reveal the "webs of significance" (p. 5) in a social and cultural situation. In doing a meta-ethnography, we are also "inscribing." The inscription is essentially written in the form of an analogy; the translations constitute the substance of the analogy. Constructing analogies and translations are familiar human enterprises and, according to Turner (1980), the essential form of social science explanation. Turner also reminds us that social researchers need to be concerned about another level of analogy, that of readers comparing their own social and cultural experiences to that revealed by research. The form of inscription used to portray a meaningful synthesis must also consider the audience in relation to the synthesis. Few analogies work for all audiences. In any case, meta-ethnographies are likely to be written. It is in the writing that the analogy and translation must fit and work (Glaser and Strauss, 1967).

Creating Analogies

A meta-ethnography requires that adequate analogies be created and that they are audience-appropriate. In practice, these are not separate operations. However, a successful synthesis does not require the analogy to be direct and complete. In fact, successful synthesis may reveal that the analogy ultimately fails and that the studies are essentially incompatible. Surface similarities may hide substantive differences in what was actually studied and/or what the accounts can be taken to mean.

The inscription of a meta-ethnography, then, is essentially in the form of analogy, either of the parts to the whole or of one account to the other. Because ethnographic accounts often are detailed and complex, it is unreasonable to conclude that a meta-ethnography is a simple analogy. The analogy itself may be judged by how well we are able to translate the accounts.

Barnwell (1980) distinguishes among three types of translations: (1) literal translations that are word-for-word translations, (2) modified literal translations that make the text grammatical in the new language, and (3) idiomatic translations that focus on translating the meaning of the text and may, therefore, substantially differ from a literal translation. In meta-ethnography, our concern is primarily with idiomatic translations. A meta-ethnographic synthesis does not involve creating a text in a new language. Rather, it entails discovering the relationships between two existing texts. For the most part, same-language studies are translated into each other. Translations are not literal, however. The individual words of one account are *not* translated into the words of the other. Rather, the translations are of the salient categories of meaning. Such idiomatic translation is what enables us to retain the holism so essential to interpretivism.

Barnwell (1980) is informative in her discussion of the problem of a concept as not being known in the language into which it is translated. She cites three alternative strategies to address this issue: (1) use a broadly descriptive phrase, so that the general meaning is conveyed; (2) use the words from the initial language for the concept, while building up as much of the context to the word/concept as possible; or (3) substitute a known concept from the language into which the original text is to be translated. In a meta-ethnography, the use of analogical comparisons takes similar forms. If the accounts to be synthesized contain untranslatable concepts, we can follow Barnwell's guidance and (1) be broadly descriptive of the similarities and differences between the concepts of the accounts; and/or (2) adapt the concepts of one text *in context* to the synthesis of both accounts.

In many ways, the effective analogy for the synthesis of interpretive accounts is one that the audience to the synthesis finds useful and insightful. Certainly meta-ethnographies can and will be written *by* qualitative researchers *for* qualitative researchers, as is the case with this book. Meta-ethnographies can also inform other audiences. Increasingly, in our utilitarian culture, that audience will be one of practitioners of some sort. An audience-appropriate meta-ethnography hopes to seize the opportunity this presents, as well as to not succumb to the threats of utilitarian culture. This is achieved by ensuring that the metaphors and analogies employed reveal the ways in which the world views of audiences are alike and dissimilar from those of the authors of the accounts. To be effective, the metaphors and analogies are to be consciously "as if," emphasizing the transfer between the audience's usual meaning and their meaning in the meta-ethnography. This, of course, implies that the synthesizer must be a student of the culture of the audience to the meta-ethnography, as well as a student of interpretivism.

Schlechty and Noblit (1982) argue that the appropriate role for the interpretivist in applied research is one of enabling dialogue between the particular audience and a more universal audience. In this we are

> obliged to push the perspectives of the universal audience with the particular audiences at the same time they push the perspectives of the particular audience with the universal audience. Thus the argument—and it should be that—is within groups and between groups [Schlechty and Noblit, 1982: 296].

Audience-appropriate meta-ethnographies focus on enabling the audience to compare their perspectives with those revealed in the studies and the synthesis. Additionally, appropriate meta-ethnographies reveal how the authors' perspective varies from that of the audience and points out the implications of such differences in world view. This can be done by inscribing the meta-ethnography as an analogy (either implicit or explicit) between the studies synthesized and the world view of the audience.

Obviously, we must know our audience and have discovered their perspectives as these relate to any synthesis. At the same time, we do not take the perspective of the audience. We serve as facilitators of the dialogue between the perspectives of the audience and the perspectives revealed in the synthesis. The entire point of approaching synthesis as a comparative translation is not to achieve closure, but to enable discourse. An audience-appropriate synthesis is one that enriches and enlarges the audience's discourse. The ideas contained in the synthesis are important, but must also engage the audience.

Expressing Synthesis

Synthesis can be expressed in various ways, drama, video, and text among them. We encourage experimentation with various media, much as the British anthropologists are experimenting with film. Nonetheless, most meta-ethnographies will be in the form of written texts. Therefore, written texts are our concern here.

Most qualitative research texts include a section on writing qualitative studies. It is important for qualitative researchers to construct adequate metaphoric translations and express the account in a way that is relevant to their audience. This level of translation was Turner's (1980) original explication of sociological explanation as translation. It is also currently being explored in anthropology (see Asad, 1986: 159).

In any form of interpretive research, there will always be a dilemma of expressing the strange in the familiar's language. This is true with meta-ethnography. In fact, because a meta-ethnography entails translation on another level—between studies—the importance of this issue is heightened. There is no technical remedy for this. As James Clifford (1986a: 6) argues: "The making of ethnography is artisanal, tied to the worldly work of writing."

For Clifford, resolution of this issue requires a "literary" ethnography that, in turn, means that in many ways the writing of ethnographies is the art of writing fiction. He explains this view of writing:

> Ethnographical writing is determined in at least six ways: (1) contextually (it draws from and creates meaningful social milieu), (2) rhetorically (it uses and is used by expressive conventions), (3) institutionally (one writes within, and against, specific traditions, disciplines, audiences), (4) generically (an ethnography is usually distinguishable from a novel or a travel account), (5) politically (the authority to represent cultural realities is unequally shared and at times contested), and (6) historically (all the above conventions and constraints are changing). These determinations govern the inscription of coherent ethnographic fictions [Clifford, 1986a: 6].

As the provocative volume by Clifford and Marcus (1986) elaborates, writing is more than just successfully making these six determinations. Howard Becker (1986) offers a more practical treatise on writing social science. He deals with a variety of organizational and stylistic issues and concludes by explaining:

> You can avoid the woolliness and pretentiousness of "classy" writing by going over your prose repeatedly, taking out words that aren't working. You can think about what kind of person you want to be in your writing and how the persona you adopt will affect the credibility of what you say. You can take your metaphors seriously and see if they still make sense. By simply *paying attention,* you can get a lot of what you do under control [Becker, 1986: 164-5].

In a sense, all ethnographic interpretation, including meta-ethnography, is allegorical (Clifford, 1986b). Our interpretations of a set of ethnographic accounts invites our readers to find the universal lessons of a particular, yet "strange," culture. The allegory is an apt way to express the lessons of the studies collected as well as to invite a range of readers to pursue them.

Allegory is an appropriate literary device for a meta-ethnography when the concern is to express the interaction of forces in some social or cultural process. Studies of educational change and program implementation seem to be appropriate for synthesis as an allegory. Moreover, allegory is particularly useful when the purpose of the meta-ethnography is to have the audience reflect about the condition, as in many evaluation situations. It may also be useful for educational purposes in general, providing direction for what is to be learned, while giving the lesson a concrete manifestation.

A caveat is necessary here. For all the efforts of an author, the meaning of one's work will be in the eyes of others. It is not possible to control how others view your work. Mead's works are now seen more allegorically than they were at the time of publication. The best we can do is to construct good translations and good analogies that work for our initial audience.

Claims about the Meaning of a Meta-Ethnography

Once the meta-ethnography is in draft form and the translations tentatively completed, a final interpretive phase beings. The interpretive issue to be resolved in this phase involves determining the meanings of the meta-ethnography for the intended audience. Some meanings simply concern understanding the world views, the ways things are done in other settings, and how these compare with those of the audience. Other meanings include a relative call to action: Something is identified that needs addressing. These meanings refer to the understandings gained from a meta-ethnography in terms of practical and technical interests (Habermas, 1971). They do not refer, however, to the meaning of synthesis in terms of the larger discourse about social and cultural life.

The meaning of a meta-ethnography in this larger sense involves our notion of the person synthesizing the studies. We view this person as a facilitator of a dialogue between the larger human discourse and the practical and technical interests of the particular audience. This, of course, implies that the person conducting the synthesis understands what this large discourse concerns. In part, this meaning is derived by placing the accounts being synthesized into the context of larger disciplinary arguments, epochal frames of thought, and so on.

This greater meaning may also be derived by the synthesizer's exploration of the implications of synthesis for the nature of knowledge. Those conducting meta-ethnographies can place these understandings in the larger discourse. In considering the implications of the synthesis, they may also find it useful to think about the various forms that the meaning of a synthesis can take. Whether the syntheses are inductive, dialectical, Kuhnian, or interdisciplinary (Strike and Posner, 1983b), they establish the relationship of the synthesis to existing knowledge bases. Although some of these are not normally consistent with an interpretative paradigm, they nevertheless can help the synthesizer reflect on the meaning of his or her synthesis.

Strike and Posner enable us to better discern what a synthesis is and is not about. Expressing an adequate synthesis and persuading an audience, however, remain the primary goals of a meta-ethnography. The nature of the synthesis is discovered in the process of the synthesis and aids, not supplants, the interpretation. Claims about its meaning will no doubt vary, for this is but one more interpretation of interpretations.

Expressing a meta-ethnographic synthesis is an involved process of writing and interpretation. It encompasses all the issues of writing good qualitative accounts plus those of writing translations and analogies. Like all modes of expression, practice, experimentation, and reflection benefit such writing.

The meaning of meta-ethnography, of course, is always in the eye of the beholder. The synthesizer may discern new insights about his or her own work or fields of study. The research may discern other analogies or other relationships between the studies—ones closer to their substantive interests. A meta-ethnography may also find its audience to be a community of discourse and as such be related to issues of concern to that community. The reflective author, reader, or community, however, will be able to see its own beliefs and everyday experiences from multiple, new perspectives. Each study is translatable into our own experience as well as into the synthesis we create. The goal of interpretivism is to enrich human discourse. Reading or conducting a meta-ethnography hopefully will enable us to participate in that discourse, to understand the issues, and to comprehend the reality of everyday life. The meta-ethnography does not do this by itself. It provides only the opportunity for us to carefully consider the relationship between studies of interest to us. If we take the opportunity provided, we and others distant from our literature(s) may be able to experience a reflective moment. In this, hopefully, we will better understand the structures of our existence and the agency we might exert.

Summary and Conclusion

A meta-ethnography is complete when we understand the meaning of the synthesis to our life and the lives of others. As we have shown, getting to this point is somewhat complex. Synthesizing qualitative research requires an interpretive approach to synthesis. We compare and synthesize qualitative accounts by writing them as analogies and translations.

Although the term *meta-ethnography* parallels *meta-analysis,* and both approaches share an interest in putting together studies, the similarity ends there. A meta-ethnography synthesizes the substance of qualitative research, while meta-analysis synthesizes the data. It is helpful to think of a meta-ethnography as any interpretive study. Studies are sought purposively to address an initial interest. The relation of studies to one another is discovered as translations are attempted. The meaning of the synthesis becomes apparent rather late in the process.

The approach to meta-ethnography we develop here is based in the more "literary" traditions of interpretivism (Clifford and Marcus, 1986). We believe it is appropriate to consider ethnographic accounts metaphorically. Given the difficulties of expressing interpretive accounts of particular audiences, we prefer to think of the key terms and concepts as metaphors rather than as literal descriptions. Further, because metaphors have cogency as well as range, they can be used to express an ethnographic account in reduced form. We call this a metaphoric reduction. We then translate these metaphoric reductions into one another. These translations are in the form of an analogy. When the analogy effects an idiomatic translation that is audience-appropriate, the synthesis is complete.

A key judgment call in meta-ethnography is the initial determination of the relation of the studies to one another. While any error becomes evident later, when translations are effected and the analogy attempted, it certainly is more efficient to consider this determination early in the synthesis process. The studies may be related to one another either as a reciprocal translation (essentially similar and subject to direct translation), as a refutation (involving translation of refutations as well as accounts), or in a line of argument (an analogy about a set of parts to some whole). Each type involves a different assumption and thus a different approach and product.

As we emphasize in this chapter, the worth of any synthesis is in its comprehensibility to some audience. The quality of the expression of the synthesis and its meaning (in terms of the larger human discourse, the discourse of the particular audience, and the dialogue between the two) is as dependent on the art of expression as it is on the substantive translations.

We hope that this monograph elicits discussion, critique, and alternative proposals. We welcome this. In meta-ethnography, as in ethnography, multiple perspectives promise us a richer and deeper understanding of our craft and our world.

REFERENCES

ASAD, T. (1986) "The concept of cultural translation in British social anthropology," in J. Clifford and G. Marcus (eds.) Writing Culture. Berkeley: University of California Press.

BARNWELL, K. (1980) Introduction to Semantics and Translation. Horsleys Green, England: Summer Institute of Linguistics.

BECKER, H. (1986) Writing for Social Scientists. Chicago: University of Chicago Press.

BERGER, P. and T. LUCKMAN (1967). The Social Construction of Reality. Garden City, NY: Doubleday.

BOSSERT, S. (1979) Task and Social Relationships in Classrooms. New York: Cambridge University Press.

BREDO, E. and W. FEINBERG [eds.] (1982). Knowledge and Values in Social and Educational Research. Philadelphia: Temple University Press.

BROWN, R. (1977) A Poetic for Sociology. New York: Cambridge University Press.

CAHEN, L. (1980) "Meta-analysis—a technique with promise and problems." Evaluation in Education 4: 37-39.

CLEMENT, D., M. EISENHART and J. HARDING (1978) The Emerging Order: An Ethnography of a Southern Desegregated School. Chapel Hill: University of North Carolina Press.

CLEMENT, D., M. EISENHART and J. HARDING (1979) "The veneer of harmony: social-race relations in a Southern desegregated school," in R. Rist (ed.) Desegregated Schools. New York: Academic Press.

CLIFFORD, J. (1986a) "Introduction: partial truths," in J. Clifford and G. Marcus (eds.) Writing Culture. Berkeley: University of California Press.

CLIFFORD, J. (1986b) "On ethnographic allegory," in J. Clifford and G. Marcus (eds.) Writing Culture. Berkeley: University of California Press.

CLIFFORD, J. and G. MARCUS [eds.] (1986c) Writing Culture. Berkeley: University of California Press.

COLLINS, T. (1979) "From courtrooms to classrooms: managing school desegregation in a Deep South high school," in R. Rist (ed.) Desegregated Schools. New York: Academic Press.

COLLINS, T. and G. NOBLIT (1978) Stratification and Resegregation: The Case of Crossover High School. Final report of NIE contract #400-76-009.

COOPER, H. (1984) The Integrative Research Review. Newbury Park, CA: Sage.

CUSICK, P. (1983) The Egalitarian Ideal and the American High School. New York: Longman.

CUSICK, P. (1985a) "Review of Reading, Writing and Resistance." Anthropology and Education Quarterly 16: 69-72.

CUSICK, P. (1985b) "Comment on the Everhart/Cusick reviews." Anthropology and Education Quarterly 16: 246-247.

84

DOUGLAS, J. (1976) Investigative Social Research. Newbury Park, CA: Sage.

EVERHART, R. (1983) Reading, Writing and Resistance. London: Routledge & Kegan Paul.

EVERHART, R. (1985a) "Review of The Egalitarian Ideal and the American High School." Anthropology and Education Quarterly 16: 73-77.

EVERHART, R. (1985b) "Comment on the Cusick/Everhart reviews." Anthropology and Education Quarterly 16: 247-248.

FREEMAN, D. (1983) Margaret Mead and Samoa. Cambridge, MA: Harvard University Press.

GEERTZ, C. (1973) The Interpretation of Cultures. New York: Basic Books.

GEERTZ, C. (1983) Local Knowledge. New York: Basic Books.

GEERTZ, C. (1984) "Anti anti-relativism." American Anthropologist 84: 263-278.

GLASER, B. and A. STRAUSS (1967) The Discovery of Grounded Theory. Chicago: Aldine.

GLASS, G. (1977) "Integrating findings: the meta-analysis of research." Review of Research in Education 5: 351-379.

GLASS, G., B. McGRAW, and M. SMITH (1981) Meta-Analysis in Social Research. Newbury Park, CA: Sage.

GOETZ, J. and M. LeCOMPTE (1984) Ethnography and Qualitative Design in Educational Research. Orlando, FL: Academic Press.

GOULDNER, A. (1970) The Coming Crisis of Western Sociology. New York: Basic Books.

HABERMAS, J. (1971) Knowledge and Human Interests. Boston, MA: Beacon Press.

HENDERSON, R. [ed.] (1981) "Effects of desegregation on white children." Urban Review 13 (4; Special issue).

HOUSE, E. (1979) "Coherence and credibility: the aesthetics of evaluation." Educational Evaluation and Policy Analysis 1 (5): 5-17.

HUNTER, J., F. SCHMIDT and G. JACKSON (1982) Meta-analysis. Newbury Park, CA: Sage.

IANNI, F. et al. (1978) A Field Study of Culture Contact and Desegregation in an Urban High School. New York: Columbia University, Teachers College, Horace-Mann—Lincoln Institute.

KUHN, T. (1970) The Structure of Scientific Revolutions. Chicago: University of Chicago Press.

LeCOMPTE, M. (1979) "Less than meets the eye," in M. Wax (ed.) Desegregated Schools: An Intimate Portrait Based on Five Ethnographic Studies. Washington, DC: National Institute of Education.

LIGHT, R. (1980) "Synthesis methods: some judgment calls that must be made. Evaluation in Education 4: 5-10.

LINCOLN, Y. and E. GUBA (1980) "The distinction between merit and worth in evaluation." Educational Evaluation and Policy Analysis, 2 (4): 61-72.

MANNHEIM, K. (1936) Ideology and Utopia. New York: Harcourt, Brace & World.

MARCUS, G. and M. FISCHER (1986) Anthropology as Cultural Critique. Chicago: University of Chicago Press.

MARSHALL, C. (1985) "Appropriate criteria of trustworthiness and goodness for qualitative research on education organizations." Quality and Quantity 19: 353-373.

MARTIN, G. (1975) Language, Truth and Poetry. Edinburgh: Edinburgh University Press.

MEAD, M. (1928) Coming of Age in Samoa. New York: William Morrow. (1964 edition)

MERTON, R. (1957) Social Theory and Social Structure. New York: Free Press.

METZ, M. (1978) Classrooms and Corridors. Los Angeles: University of California Press.

MILES, M. and A. HUBERMAN (1984) Qualitative Data Analysis. Newbury Park, CA: Sage.

MILLS, C. W. (1959) The Sociological Imagination. New York: Oxford University Press.

MISHLER, E. (1979) "Meaning in context." Harvard Educational Review 119 (1): 1-19.

NOBLIT, G. (1979) "Patience and prudence in a Southern high school," in R. Rist (ed.) Desegregated Schools. New York: Academic Press.

NOBLIT, G. (1981) "The holistic alternative in policy research." High School Journal 65 (2): 43-49.

NOBLIT, G. (1984) "The prospects of an applied ethnography for education: a sociology of knowledge interpretation." Educational Evaluation and Policy Analysis 6 (1): 95-101.

NOBLIT, G. and B. JOHNSON [eds.] (1982) The School Principal and School Desegregation. Springfield, IL: Charles C. Thomas.

PATTON, M. (1975) Alternative Evaluation Research Paradigm. North Dakota Study Group on Evaluation Monograph Series. Grand Forks: University of North Dakota.

PATTON, M. (1980) Qualitative Evaluation Methods. Newbury Park, CA: Sage.

RIST, R. (1979) Desegregated Schools: Appraisals of an American Experiment. New York: Academic Press.

ROSENBAUM, P. (1979) "Five perspectives on desegregation in schools: a summary," in M. Wax (ed.) When Schools are Desegregated. Washington, DC: National Institute of Education.

SAGAR, A. and J. SCHOFIELD (1979) "Integrating the desegregated school: perspectives, practices, and possibilities," in M. Wax (ed.) When Schools are Desegregated. Washington, DC: National Institute of Education.

SCHERER, J. and E. SLAWSKI (1978) Hard Walls-Soft Walls: The Social Ecology of an Urban Desegregated High School. Rochester, MI: Oakland University Press.

SCHERER, J. and E. SLAWSKI (1979) "Color, class, and social control in an urban desegregated school," in R. Rist (ed.) Desegregated Schools. New York: Academic Press.

SCHLECHTY, P. and G. NOBLIT (1982) "Some uses of sociological theory in educational evaluation," in R. Corwin (ed.) Policy Research. Greenwich, CT: JAI Press.

SCHOFIELD, J. and A. SAGAR (1978) Social Process and Peer Relations in a "Nearly Desegregated" Middle School. Pittsburgh, PA: University of Pittsburgh.

SCHOFIELD, J. and A. SAGAR (1979) "The social context of learning in an interracial school," in R. Rist (ed.) Desegregated Schools. New York: Academic Press.

SHANKMAN, P. (1984) "The thick and the thin: on the interpretive theoretical program of Clifford Geertz." Current Anthropology 25 (3): 261-280.

SPICER, E. (1976) "Beyond analysis and explanation." Human Organization 35 (4): 335-343.

STRIKE, K. and G. POSNER (1983a) "Epistemological problems in organizing social science knowledge for application," in S. Ward and L. Reed (eds.) Knowledge Structure and Use. Philadelphia: Temple University Press.

STRIKE, K. and G. POSNER (1983b) "Types of syntheses and their criteria," in S. Ward and L. Reed (eds.) Knowledge Structure and Use. Philadelphia: Temple University Press.

SULLIVAN, M. (1979a) "The community context of five desegregated schools," in M. Wax (ed.) When Schools Are Desegregated. Washington, DC: National Institute of Education.

SULLIVAN M. (1979b) "Contacts among cultures: school desegregation in a polyethnic New York City high school," in R. Rist (ed.) Desegregated Schools. New York: Academic Press.

TAYLOR, C. (1982) "Interpretation and the sciences of man," in E. Bredo and W. Feinberg (eds.) Knowledge and Values in Social and Educational Research. Philadelphia: Temple University Press.

TURNER, S. (1980) Sociological Explanation as Translation. New York: Cambridge University Press.

WARD, S. (1983) "Knowledge structure and knowledge synthesis," in S. Ward and L. Reed (eds.) Knowledge Structures and Use. Philadelphia: Temple University Press.

WAX, M. (1979a) Desegregated Schools: An Intimate Portrait Based on Five Ethnographic Studies. Washington, DC: National Institute of Education.

WAX, M. (1979b) When Schools Are Desegregated. Washington, DC: National Institute of Education.

WINCH, P. (1958) The Idea of a Social Science and Its Relation to Philosophy. Atlantic Highlands, NJ: Humanities Press.

WOLCOTT, H. (1973) The Man in the Principal's Office. New York: Holt, Rinehart & Winston.

WOLCOTT, H. (1980) "How to look like an anthropologist without really being one." Practicing Anthropology 3 (2): 56-59.

YIN, R. (1984) Case Study Research: Design and Methods. Newbury Park, CA: Sage.

ABOUT THE AUTHORS

George W. Noblit is Associate Professor of Social Foundations of Education and Clinical Associate Professor of Family Medicine at the University of North Carolina at Chapel Hill. His current investigations include a sociology of knowledge analysis of evaluation research and the literary tradition of ethnographic research. From 1973 to 1979, he was Assistant and then Associate Professor of Sociology at Memphis State University. He was a Senior Fellow with the National Institute of Education, and an Educational Policy Fellow at the Institute of Educational Leadership. In 1984, he was Lecturer in the Department of Education, Massey University (New Zealand), and, with his wife, toured New Zealand by bicycle.

Dr. Noblit teaches sociology of education, organizational theory, and qualitative research methods in the School of Education at The University of North Carolina. He teaches and advises research in various faculty preparation programs in the Department of Family Medicine and the Office of Research and Development for Education in the Health Professions in the School of Medicine. He is author of many articles and book chapters, and is the coeditor of two volumes of original qualitative studies: *The Social Context of Schooling* (Ablex, 1987) with William Pink, and *The School Principal and School Desegregation* (Charles Thomas, 1982) with William Johnston. He received his M.S. and Ph.D. in sociology from the University of Oregon.

R. Dwight Hare is Assistant Professor at Northeast Louisiana University and teaches in the Department of Administration, Supervision, and Foundations, College of Education. He teaches education foundations courses, classroom evaluation and measurement, statistics, and finance. He was awarded the Ph.D. by the University of North Carolina at Chapel Hill in 1984.

Dr. Hare's primary research interests involve the use of qualitative research methods in evaluation and policy analysis. His recent studies include an examination of the Nursing and Medical Scholarship

Programs of the Richland Parish (LA) Hospital System; investigation of the career intentions and mobility patterns of freshman academic scholarship recipients; investigations of the career intentions and mobility patterns of teacher education majors; evaluation of a drop-out prevention program of Monroe (LA) City Schools; and investigations of the employment and mobility patterns of specialty teachers in a rural Louisiana school system. His specific areas of interest are the many aspects of the teacher labor market, particularly as they relate to rural and small schools. His publications include "The Dynamics of the Teacher Labor Market" (*High School Journal*), "Staff Development Needs Assessment" (*Catalyst for Change*), "Evaluation of a Preservice Teacher Education Program" (*LERJ*), and "A Qualitative Critique of Teacher Labor Market Studies" (*Urban Review*). He is an Invited Juror of the *National Forum of Educational Administration and Supervision Journal.*